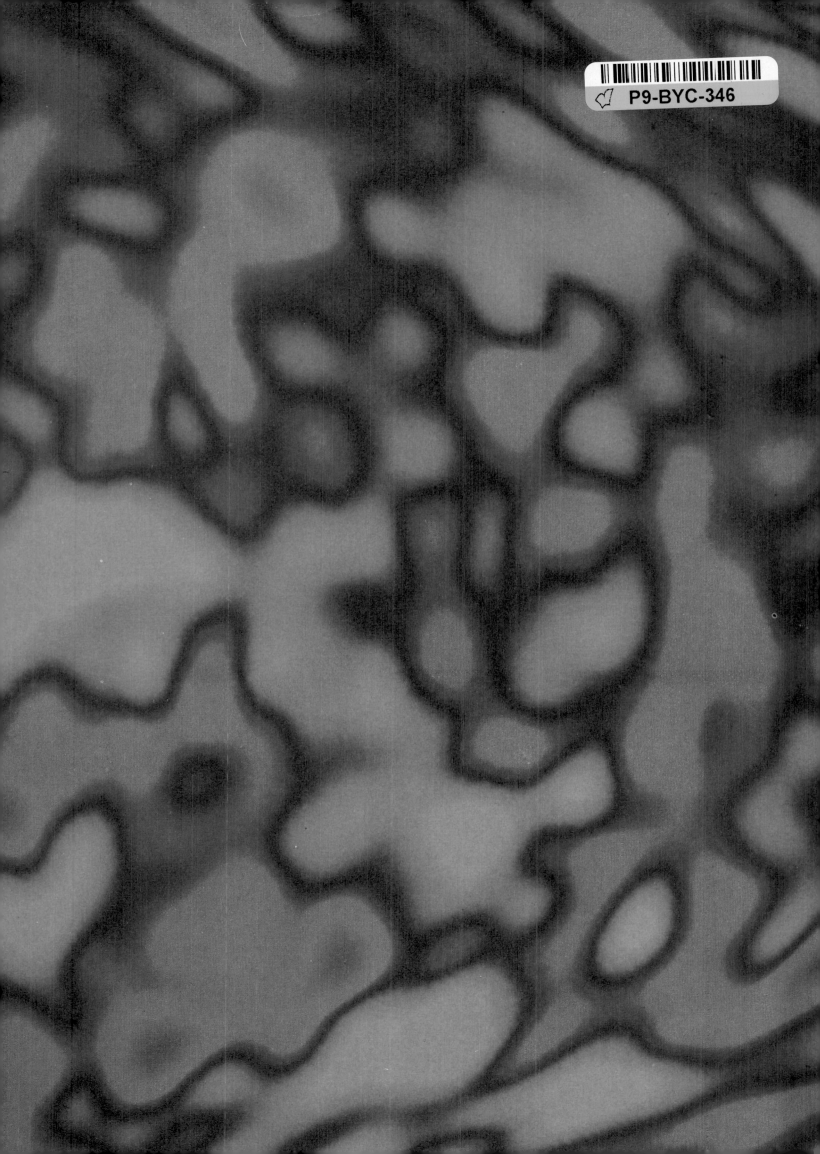

Big Bang

Heather Couper and Nigel Henbest

Illustrated by Luciano Corbella

A DK PUBLISHING BOOK

Editor   Jackie Wilson
Art Editor   Martyn Foote
US Editor   Camela Decaire
Deputy Editorial Director   Sophie Mitchell
Deputy Art Director   Miranda Kennedy
DTP Designer   Andrew O'Brien
Production   Charlotte Traill
Picture researcher   Julia Harris-Voss

First American Edition, 1997
2 4 6 8 10 9 7 5 3 1

Published in the United States by DK Publishing, Inc.
95 Madison Avenue, New York, NY 10016
Visit us on the World Wide Web at http:/www.dk.com

Published in Great Britain by Dorling Kindersley Ltd.

A catalog record for this book is available from the Library of Congress.

ISBN 0-7894-1484-8

Reproduced by Colourscan, Singapore
Printed in Italy by L.E.G.O.

Contents

8   Countdown

10   T equals zero

12   Blowup

14   Particle soup

16   Creation of matter

18   First elements

20   Echoes of the Big Bang

22   Ripples in space

24   Birth of the Milky Way

26   Creation myths

28   Unfolding Universe

32 Scale of space

34 Galaxies on the move

36 How old is the Universe?

38 Curved cosmos

40 Far future

42 Other big bangs

44 Glossary

45 Index

This book follows the story of the Universe all the way from its birth to the present — and beyond. Each successive spread relates the next stage in the unfolding saga, so it is best to read the book in sequence. For a compact history, turn to pages 28-31.

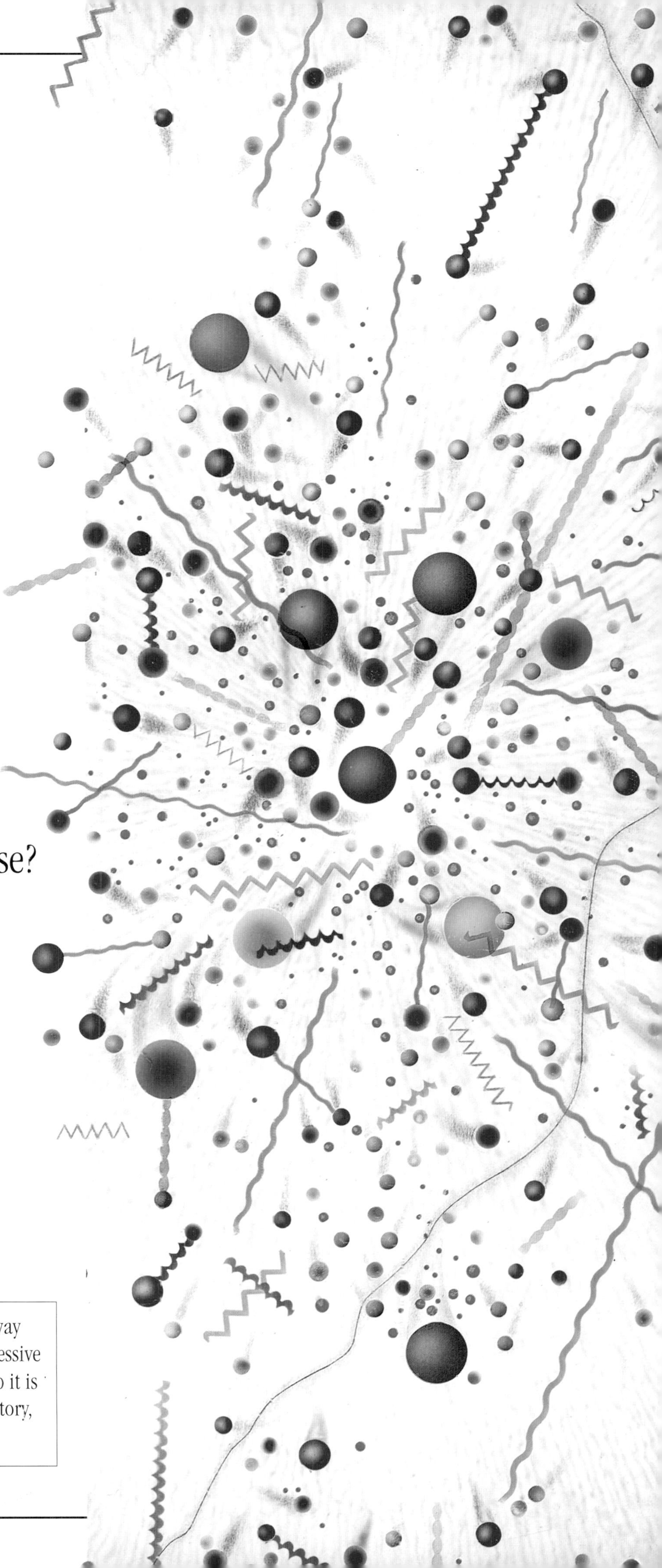

Countdown

IN THE BEGINNING, THERE WAS NOTHING. It was a "nothing" so profound it defies human comprehension. We may think of the emptiest parts of the Universe today – out in the cold realms between the distant galaxies – as "nothing regions." But even they contain a sprinkling of atoms, and the faint radiation of dim shafts of light passing through. More fundamentally, the emptiest regions today are supported by the invisible structure of space, and respond to the inaudible clock of time. A long, long time ago, there was no matter, and no radiation. More importantly, space did not exist; time did not flow. Our story begins "once upon a time" – when there was no space, and there was no time.

No time
Time is not an ever-rolling stream, flowing from forever in the past to forever in the future. The flow of time is intimately linked to space – and to matter and gravity. We cannot speak of what happened before the Big Bang, because time itself did not exist then.

No space
Before space was created, nothing could exist; there was nowhere for it to exist in. Our Universe probably came into existence not only from nothing, but from nowhere.

Why?
Science cannot answer the question of why the Universe began. Why didn't the original "nothing" stay that way? Philosophers and theologians have their own answers, which can probably never be proven one way or the other. All we do know is that something did happen.

T equals zero

FROM NOTHING, a tiny speck of brilliant light appeared. It was almost infinitely hot. Inside this fireball was all of space. With the creation of space came the birth of time: the great cosmic clock began to tick some 13 billion years ago. The energy in the fireball was so concentrated that matter spontaneously started to appear: a distant ancestor of the matter that would later become the building blocks of stars, planets, and galaxies. The infant Universe hit the ground running. As soon as the fireball appeared, it started expanding – not into anything, but throughout, because the Universe was, and is, everything and everywhere. In the first trillion-trillion-trillionth of a second, shown here, the Universe grew a hundred million times bigger, and its temperature dropped from near infinity to 10,000 trillion trillion degrees.

DAWN OF TIME

There was no "before" the Big Bang, because time did not exist. When there was no space and no matter, there was no such thing as time either. Cosmologists believe space and time are intimately linked. Once time existed, space could start to expand; once space was created, time was able to flow.

The Big Bang took place about 13 billion years ago.

ORIGINS OF SPACE

The Big Bang was not an explosion *into* anything – it happened everywhere: there was no surrounding empty space. Space itself was created at the instant of the Big Bang. Astronomers see the aftermath of creation all around us today in the continued expansion of the Universe. The galaxies – "star cities" – appear to be rushing away from each other at high speeds. But in reality, it is the space between the galaxies that is stretching, carrying them apart.

A small fragment of the Universe begins to expand.

The growing Universe starts to cool, changing color and growing dimmer.

In reality, the temperature of the infant Universe is so high that it always appears blindingly bright during this period.

RECREATING THE BIG BANG

When scientists investigate the origin of the Universe, their tools are not telescopes, but particle accelerators. The closest they can come to the very early Universe is to re-create its searingly diabolic conditions in high-energy accelerators, where powerful electrical fields accelerate particles such as electrons until they are traveling very close to the velocity of light, nature's ultimate speed limit. When these particles smash head-on in a paroxysm of energy, an exotic array of subatomic particles fleetingly appears, only to disappear fractions of a second later. Such particles were commonly found in the early days of the Big Bang.

The Big Bang revisited: these are tracks from particles, created in an accelerator, that are rarely found in today's Universe.

As space expands, the density rapidly falls. It starts at an incredible 10 billion trillion trillion trillion trillion trillion trillion grams per cubic inch.

Even the most sophisticated theories cannot tell us what happened at the exact instant of creation. The earliest we can wind the clock back to is 10 million-trillion-trillion-trillionths of a second after creation.

The separation of time from space liberated space, allowing the creation and expansion of the Universe.

The raging inferno

The infant Universe was searingly hot, brimming with the energy of intense radiation. Albert Einstein's famous equation $E=mc^2$ says that mass and energy are interchangeable: one can be turned into the other. In the early Universe, the energy of the radiation was so intense that it could spontaneously turn into "lumps" of matter. These took the form of subatomic particles, such as electrons, and their antimatter partners, such as positrons. Antimatter has exactly the opposite properties of matter. If the two meet, they destroy, or annihilate, each other. The particles and antiparticles lasted just fractions of a second before annihilating each other in a burst of energy that converted them back to radiation – which then created more matter-antimatter pairs.

A SMALL MATTER OF CREATION

The phrase "Big Bang" is not a very accurate one. The Universe actually started with a rather small – not to say puny – bang. Even the amount of energy involved in the expansion was rather paltry. If converted into matter, it would amount to only about 2 lb (1 kg), or the equivalent of a bag of sugar.

The fledgling Universe does not contain matter as we know it, or familiar forces like gravity. Instead, matter, radiation, and forces are jumbled together in a totally unfamiliar tangle.

MICROSCOPIC CAULDRON

If you could take a microscope to the early Universe, it would appear as a seething cauldron of radiation and subatomic particles forever appearing and disappearing.

Particles can literally materialize from a momentary concentration of energy. The result is a pair of subatomic particles, one made of matter, the other antimatter.

The particles and antiparticles try to fly apart, but in the dense fireball they quickly meet up again.

As they collide, the particles and antiparticles annihilate each other in a flash of radiation. This energy returns to the seething pool of radiation in the fireball in a continuing cycle of creation and annihilation.

GHOSTLY PARTICLES

Even in a vacuum, matter and antimatter can spontaneously appear. A pair of particles and antiparticles can materialize by "borrowing" energy from the vacuum. They are known as virtual particles because they must annihilate themselves almost immediately and return the energy debt.

SMALL AND LIFELESS

If the Universe had continued to expand like this, it would have ended up small, sparse – and lifeless. But something amazing happened…

Blowup

SUDDENLY, THE UNIVERSE BLEW UP! In practically no time at all, it grew a hundred trillion trillion trillion trillion times. And its once searing temperature dropped to almost zero. This phenomenal growth is called "cosmic inflation." In comparison, the original Big Bang was about as spectacular as a hand grenade going off in a nuclear war. As quickly as it had started, inflation came to an end. Now the temperature shot up again and particles of matter and antimatter appeared. Inflation solves many problems that the straightforward Big Bang theory cannot answer. It explains why the Universe is so big and smooth, why different forces act in it today, and where the vast amount of matter came from.

INVENTOR OF INFLATION
In 1979, Alan Guth was a particle physicist, at the Stanford Linear Accelerator Center in California, interested in how the forces might be unified – the "Grand Unified Theory." His calculations led to the idea of cosmic inflation. Since then, Guth's theory of inflation has answered more questions about the Universe than he originally sought to answer.

Alan Guth was only 32 when he devised his theory of inflation.

Cosmic inflation

The young Universe contained more energy than it knew what to do with, and it entered a period of instability. One effect of this was to fuel a dramatic growth spurt. Between ten trillion-trillion-trillionths of a second and ten billion-trillion-trillionths of a second (usually written 10^{-35} and 10^{-32} seconds – see Glossary) after the Big Bang, the Universe underwent a dramatic period of inflation. The end result was not only a Universe 100 trillion trillion trillion trillion times bigger, but the creation of the vast amounts of matter that fill the Universe today.

An instant after creation, the Universe is almost infinitely hot and expanding very slowly.

This portion shown here contains only enough energy to make 2 lb (1 kg) of matter and measures 10^{-23} inch across, far smaller than an atom.

Had inflation not happened, the Universe might have collapsed back on itself and self-destructed – after existing for less than a second.

The young Universe cools as it expands.

Pre-inflation, the Universe has a temperature of 10^{28} degrees, or 10,000 trillion trillion degrees.

As the temperature drops to below 10^{28} degrees, the Universe suddenly inflates. It doubles its size every 10^{-34} seconds, rapidly cooling as it does so.

Why the Universe we live in is so smooth

If inflation had not happened, the Universe we see today (within the sphere) would be like a patchwork quilt of different regions. Instead, the Universe is very uniform.

Inflation had the effect of expanding each region of the early Universe so that it became immense. We are well inside one region, so our neighborhood appears uniform.

Today, the Universe is incredibly smooth: wherever astronomers look in the Universe, they see the same kinds of galaxies and measure the same background temperature. This is a problem for cosmologists, who predict that different portions of space in the Big Bang would have had slightly differing temperatures and densities. These would have grown into a patchwork of diverse regions in the Universe around us. The theory of inflation offers a way out. Each original portion from the Big Bang has grown immensely larger than the Universe we can see, so our observable Universe lies entirely within just one of these regions.

The few existing particles and antiparticles are scattered far and wide, so the enormously expanded Universe is an almost perfect vacuum.

Although the Universe is effectively a vacuum, it is packed with pairs of virtual particles, which are continually appearing and disappearing.

By the end of inflation – 10^{-32} seconds after the Big Bang – the temperature has fallen to almost absolute zero (0 Kelvin, which is $-460°F$ or $-273°C$).

THE FORCE BEHIND INFLATION

Before inflation, the Universe had only two forces – gravity and a unified "superforce." This superforce permeated the regions of vacuum that lay between the jostling particles and antiparticles. When the temperature dropped to 10^{28} degrees, the superforce should have split up. But the vacuum state became "hung," just as supercooled water can stay liquid below its freezing point. This unstable supercooled state tipped the Universe into uncontrollable inflation.

You can cool pure water below freezing, and it stays liquid…

…but when supercooled water does freeze, it does so instantly – releasing energy.

Gravity was the first to separate from the unified superforce.

Gravity

Strong force

The strong force separated next, followed by the weak force.

Weak force

Electromagnetic force

SEPARATION

Today, matter in the Universe feels four different forces, but before inflation, three of these were a unified "superforce." When they started separating, the change released a huge surge of energy, which materialized as particles. So the separation of the forces created the first matter.

A surge of energy at the end of inflation sets the virtual particles and antiparticles free to lead independent existences.

Inflation created practically all the mass in the Universe today: that's why Guth calls it the "ultimate free lunch."

All the time, virtual particles and antiparticles are spontaneously appearing and then disappearing in an instant as they annihilate each other.

Get real!

By 10^{-32} seconds, the separation of the forces had boosted the temperature from zero back to 10^{28} degrees and flooded the Universe with energy. So when virtual particle and antiparticle pairs came into being, there was no need to pay off the energy debt by instantly annihilating each other. The two particles absorbed the spare energy and were free to go their own ways. And so, from being virtual, matter got real – and the mass of the Universe increased from 2 lb (1 kg) to the 10^{50} tons (tonnes) it contains today.

During a brief unstable period, inflation works like antigravity, driving everything apart.

EXTENT OF INFLATION

During the brief period when the Universe was "stuck" in its vacuum state, it ballooned in size very rapidly. A comparison with objects we know today gives an idea of this enormous expansion: a region far smaller than an atom blew up to become larger than the biggest galaxy. Some scientists say the period of cosmic inflation really deserves to be called the "Big Bang."

From smaller than an atom to bigger than a galaxy: that's how much the Universe grew during the brief period of inflation.

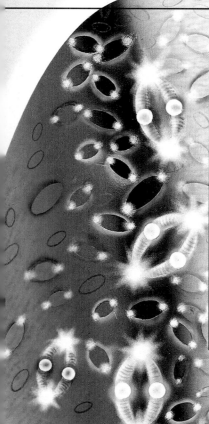

Particle soup

HOT ON THE HEELS OF ITS DRAMATIC INFLATION, the Universe embarked on the most frenetic period in its entire history. Fueled by the tremendous surge of energy released, it launched itself into an orgy of matter creation. Many of the particles forged in that inferno no longer exist. In this early phase, when it was all of ten billion-trillion-trillionths of a second old, the Universe experimented with exotic creations that rapidly decayed or changed into other particles. This era was one of total turmoil. The scene must have looked like a view through an out-of-control kaleidoscope, or a movie of fish swarming around a coral reef in fast forward.

Magnetic monopole: Heavy particle with only one magnetic pole (ordinary magnets have two) predicted by the Grand Unified Theory. It is thought to determine the electric charge of other particles, such as quarks and electrons.

Leptons: Lightweight particles such as electrons that are sensitive to the weak force.

Snapshot of a subatomic world

An enormously magnified snapshot of the Universe would reveal an intensely hot "soup" of seething subatomic particles and antiparticles (shown as solid and semi-solid spheres, respectively). Some are still around today, while others have disappeared. Quarks, leptons, WIMPs, cosmic strings, and primordial black holes cannoned around like tiny billiard balls. Gluons, W and Z bosons, and gravitons – which are found today mainly as "messengers" carrying the forces – then existed as real particles.

WIMPs: Weakly interacting massive particles that may comprise most of the dark matter believed to make up 90 percent of the mass of the present-day Universe.

Quark: Today, these are the building blocks of protons and neutrons in the nuclei of atoms. There are six known varieties, or "flavors."

W or Z boson

The weak force, governed by W and Z bosons, controls the energy of the Sun.

Gluon

W and Z bosons: *Particles, similar to the photon but with mass, that convey the weak force.*

THE FOUR FORCES

The four fundamental forces we know today have vastly different strengths, and affect different particles. Gravity, by far the weakest, influences all particles, while the most powerful, the strong force, works only inside the nucleus of atoms. At high energies, the strong force weakens, while the electromagnetic and weak forces grow stronger. Physicists believe they were once all one force (but separate from gravity). This is the Grand Unified Theory, which predicts the existence of X bosons and cosmic strings.

The strong force, carried by gluons, makes an atom bomb explode.

Photon

Graviton: *The particle thought to convey gravitational force, although it has not yet been detected.*

Photons, conveyed by the electromagnetic force, drive communications.

Graviton

Gravity, thought to be conveyed by gravitons, pulls free-fall parachutists to Earth.

Gluon: *the particle that carries the strong force, which pulls quarks together.*

Cosmic string: *An incredibly thin yet absurdly heavy strand of energy whose existence has been predicted by some theories. Cosmic strings millions of light-years long may have "seeded" the formation of galaxies.*

QUARKS AND LEPTONS: THE SURVIVORS

Although the early Universe contained many massive particles, the lightweight particles were the survivors, and are still around today. Atoms – the basic units that make up all the matter around us – are built up of quarks and leptons. Three quarks apiece make up each proton and neutron in the central nucleus of an atom. The positively charged nucleus is balanced by the negative electrons (a type of lepton) swarming around it.

Quarks can combine in threes to build protons, which are positively charged, or neutrons, with no electrical charge.

An antiquark, made of anti-matter, has the opposite properties of a quark. If the two meet, they annihilate each other.

The best-known type of lepton is an electron, a tiny particle that today swarms around atomic nuclei.

Antileptons are the antimatter equivalent of leptons. The electron's opposite is a positron.

Primordial black hole: *A mini black hole, the size of an atom but as heavy as a mountain. The British physicist Stephen Hawking believes that many were created in the early Universe, but none have yet been found.*

Neutrino: *The second most common particle in the Universe. Neutrinos are leptons, and come in three varieties. They are so lightweight that their mass has yet to be measured. If they had even a small mass, neutrinos could make up the dark matter in the Universe.*

NEUTRINO ASTRONOMY

Every second, a hundred billion neutrinos from the Big Bang pass through your body. They have survived unchanged from the era of "particle soup": by studying them, scientists could check their theories of the earliest moments of the Universe. Unfortunately, neutrinos are difficult to catch. Physicists have detected some from the Sun and a supernova, but none so far from the Big Bang.

Inside a "neutrino telescope" in New Mexico

X boson: *The heaviest particle of all, predicted by the Grand Unified Theory but as yet undetected. It would have the power to change quarks into leptons (and vice versa).*

Antiparticle —

Higgs boson: *A very heavy particle proposed by British physicist Peter Higgs. He believes it is associated with a field (the "Higgs Field") that serves to give particles mass.*

Photon: *Massless particle that transmits light and other radiation, and also conveys the electromagnetic force. The photon is the most common particle in the Universe.*

Particle

Creation of matter

THE UNIVERSE BECAME A BATTLEGROUND as it entered its next phase. It was thronged with subatomic particles of all kinds fighting for supremacy, and there was also constant warfare between equally matched battalions of matter and antimatter. A particle and its antiparticle counterpart would inevitably meet up and destroy one another. The radiation produced in these skirmishes helped fuel the action, providing the energy to create still more particle-antiparticle pairs. But by the time the Universe was a second old, all was quiet: antimatter had been vanquished and matter ruled.

COOLING CONDITIONS

The Universe changed dramatically between 10^{-32} and 1 second. As the relentless expansion continued, the Universe cooled. In the hot, early stages, massive particles and antiparticles were common. By the end of the era, when temperatures had dropped to 10 billion degrees, most of the massive particles had gone, antimatter had all but disappeared, and quarks were ganging up to make the matter we know today.

The X boson and its counterpart, the anti-X, soon disappear. The temperature rapidly drops too low to create particles this heavy. The existing X bosons and anti-Xs are unstable, and decay into showers of leptons, quarks, and their antiparticles.

PERIOD OF CHANGE

Throughout this period, the Universe was a turmoil of annihilation, decay, and the creation of new matter-antimatter pairs. Here we highlight just a few of the most important milestones.

W and Z bosons decay into lighter particles. From now on, they appear only as messenger particles that convey the weak force between quarks and leptons. Scientists first re-created W and Z bosons at the CERN particle accelerator laboratory in Switzerland in 1983.

The richness of the original exotic particle soup quickly turned into a thin gruel of more homely particles as the Universe expanded and cooled.

A BIAS TOWARD MATTER

The power of inflation created exactly equal amounts of matter and antimatter. So why didn't they wipe each other out? The answer may lie with the massive X boson and its counterpart, the anti-X. As the Universe cooled, the X and anti-X both decayed into lighter particles and antiparticles (quarks and leptons). But both kinds of decay slightly favored matter: for every 100,000,000 quarks and leptons created, there were only 99,999,999 antiquarks and antileptons. This tiny imbalance has resulted in the stars, planets, and galaxies that populate our Universe today.

X-boson decays into…

Anti-X decays into…

Particles *Anti-particles* *Particles* *Anti-particles*

But there are slightly more particles than antiparticles.

SEARCHING FOR ANTIMATTER

How do we know that some objects in the Universe are *not* made of antimatter? The answer is that every part of space is in contact with its neighboring region. If a region of antimatter existed, astronomers would detect flashes of radiation at its boundary, where the anti-atoms met up with ordinary atoms in the adjacent region. Astronomers have looked for such telltale radiation without success.

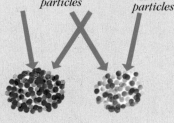

An Andromeda Galaxy made of antimatter would look the same as one made of matter. The same goes for humans – but beware of shaking hands with your antimatter counterpart!

Annihilation and decay

Particles were constantly disappearing: they were either annihilated on meeting their antiparticles or decayed into lighter particles. Meanwhile, particle-antiparticle pairs were being regenerated from the intense radiation all around. But as the Universe cooled, it could no longer make the heaviest particle-antiparticle pairs, and they became extinct.

A millionth of a second after the Big Bang, the temperature drops so low that the radiation can no longer create quark-antiquark pairs. The remaining antiquarks annihilate with the more numerous quarks, leaving a small residue of quarks.

A FAMILY OF QUARKS

The quark family got its name from a quote in James Joyce's book *Finnegans Wake*: "Three quarks for Mr. Mark." There are six quarks (three pairs): from heaviest to lightest they are top and bottom, charm and strange, and up and down. All quarks carry an electric charge: some are positive (such as the up quark) and some negative (such as the down quark). Only the two lightest quarks are stable — the others decay into down and up quarks.

Top   Bottom

Charm   Strange

Down   Up

Today, quarks live in twos or threes. This up-down-up arrangement is a positively charged proton.

The slightly heavier down-up-down arrangement is a neutron. The quarks are held together by gluons.

The lightest antiparticles, the antileptons, survive longer than any other kind of antimatter. The remaining antileptons annihilated with the more numerous leptons, leaving a small residue of leptons.

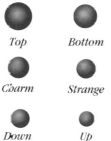

The first multiple particles, made of three quarks joined together by gluons, come together one ten-thousandth of a second after the Big Bang. These composite particles are protons and neutrons, which will form the nuclei of today's atoms.

Although the neutrinos and WIMPs will never make up atoms, planets, or stars, they will become crucial players in the Universe. WIMPs or neutrinos, or both, may form the dark matter, which controls the motion of galaxies and dictates the ultimate fate of the Universe with its gravity.

LIGHTEST LASTS LONGEST

Leptons are lightweight particles (lepton is taken from the Greek word for "light"). There are six types of leptons: the tau, the muon, and the electron, and their associated neutrinos. Leptons can have an electric charge (for example, the electron), or none at all. Tau and muon leptons are unstable, and eventually decay into electrons and neutrinos. All three types of neutrinos are stable.

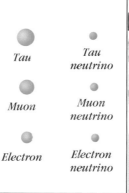

Tau   Tau neutrino

Muon   Muon neutrino

Electron   Electron neutrino

The survivors

The building blocks of matter today — protons, neutrons, and electrons — were a minor constituent of the Universe at the age of one second. All around, in vast numbers, were neutrinos. Surviving among these lightweight particles, there may have been massive remnants of the past: WIMPS, magnetic monopoles, cosmic strings, and primordial black holes. But above all, there was light. Photons (particles of light and other radiation, such as gamma rays) outnumbered matter particles by 100 million to one.

First elements

COMPARED WITH AN INSTANT before, the one-second-old Universe was a model of restraint. Nevertheless, it seethed with activity – busier than it would be at any period in the next few hundred thousand years. Packed with dazzling photons, neutrinos, and WIMPs, rushing around in temperatures of 10 billion degrees, there was also a minuscule number of protons, neutrons, and electrons. Over the next three minutes, the expanding cosmos cooled into a place where construction could begin. By the end of the third minute, the basic building blocks – the protons and neutrons – had created the kind of matter we would recognize today, the first three elements.

Cosmic oven

The young Universe had a head start in creating elements because some of its protons would become the nuclei of the simplest element, hydrogen. But it had only the briefest of times to build anything more complex. Before the first second, conditions were just too energetic: intense radiation zapped apart fragile partnerships between protons and neutrons. And after three minutes, the relentless expansion of the Universe drove would-be coalitions of particles apart. Between these extremes, the environment was just right for cooking up the nuclei of the elements helium and lithium.

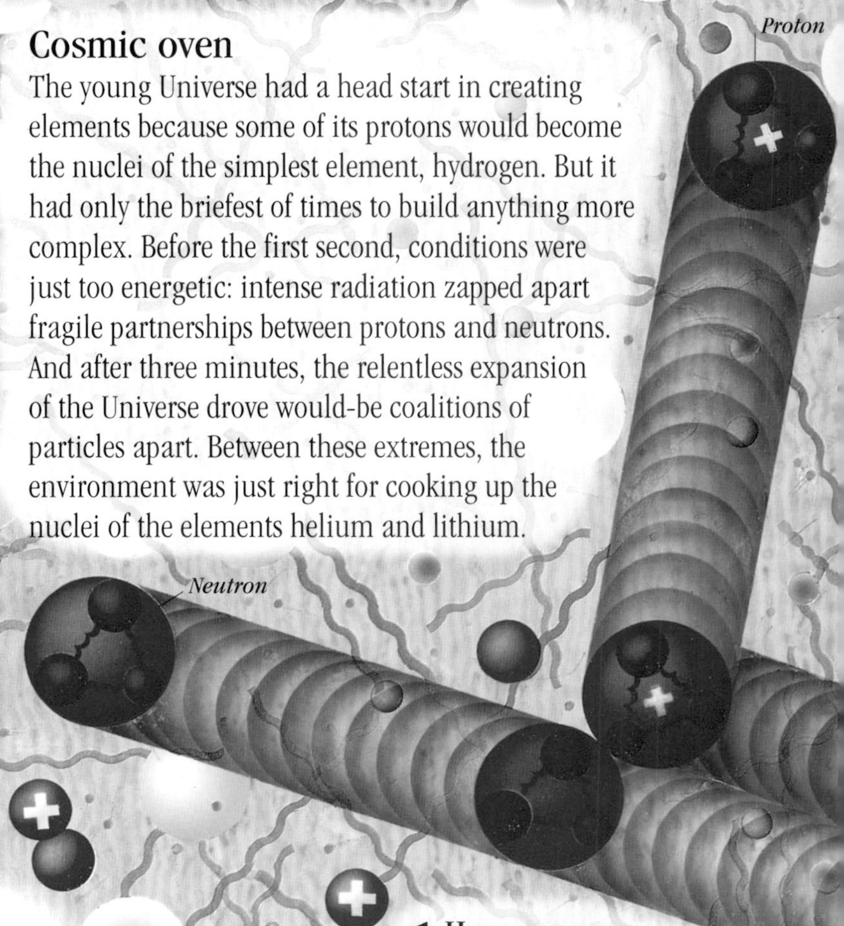

Proton

Neutron

Neutron with two down quarks and one up

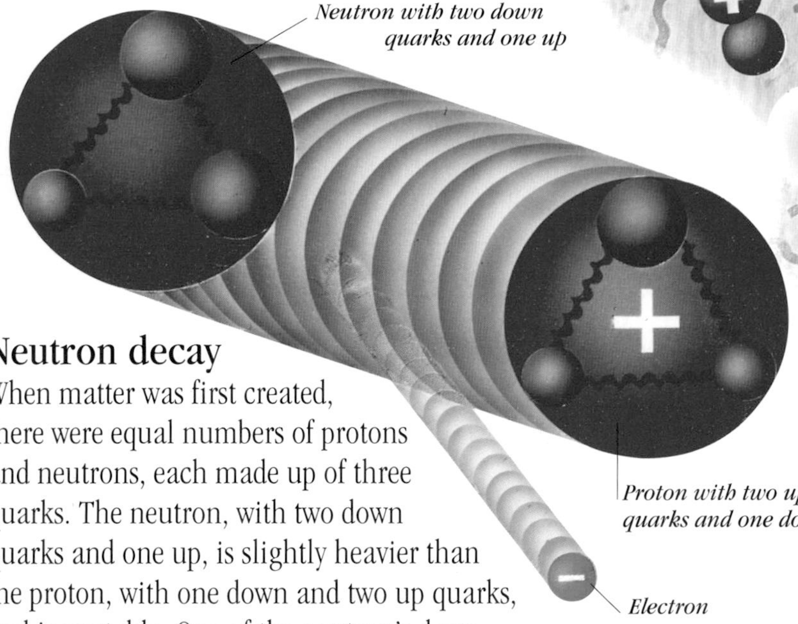

Neutron decay

When matter was first created, there were equal numbers of protons and neutrons, each made up of three quarks. The neutron, with two down quarks and one up, is slightly heavier than the proton, with one down and two up quarks, and is unstable. One of the neutron's down quarks decays into an up, giving off a negatively charged electron and a neutral antineutrino (not shown here) in the process. The result is that the neutron turns into a proton.

Proton with two up quarks and one down

Electron

1 HEAVY HYDROGEN
A proton and a neutron combine to create a nucleus of "heavy hydrogen," hydrogen-2 or deuterium. Some deuterium nuclei escape further reactions and are still found in the Universe today.

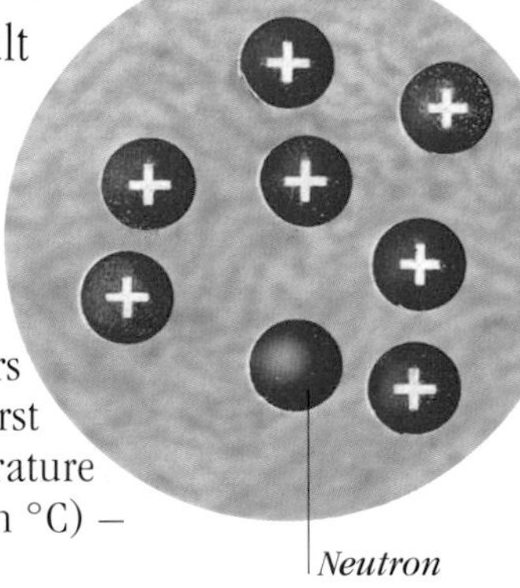

COSMIC MASTER CHEF

To Russian-American physicist George Gamow – who conceived the Big Bang theory as we now know it – the early Universe was a primordial cauldron. In the late 1940s, he and his colleagues proposed that the elements were created during a very early period of the expanding Universe. They also predicted that there would be an "afterglow" arising from this hot, early phase, bathing the whole Universe. The prediction was forgotten – until the afterglow was discovered almost 20 years later.

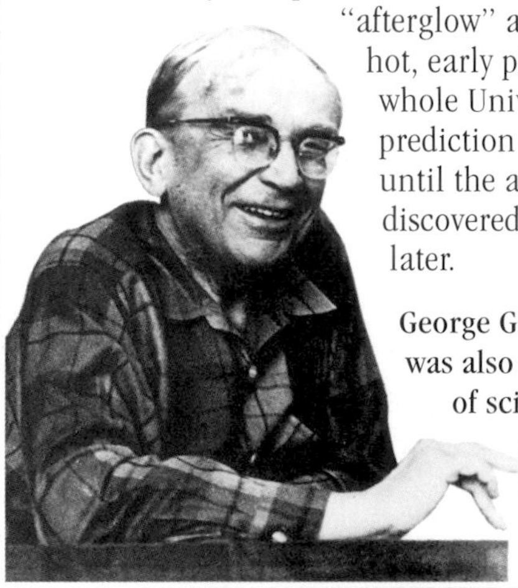

George Gamow (1904-1968) was also a great popularizer of science, wrote poetry, and did research in genetics.

PROTONS ON THE RAMPAGE

At the end of the first second, neutrons began to decay into protons. Proton numbers went on the increase, and by the time the first elements started to form – when the temperature had cooled to 1,600 million °F (900 million °C) – there were seven protons to every neutron.

Neutron

The electrons, neutrinos, radiation, and WIMPs do not play an active role in building the elements, but they are still very much present.

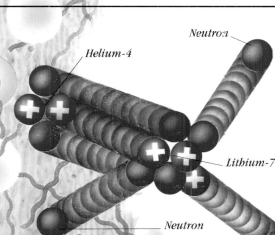

Neutron

Helium-4

Lithium-7

Neutron

Proton

4 LAST AND LEAST — LITHIUM

By the end of the first three minutes, the frenzy of element creation is almost over. There is just time for one final reaction. A few helium-4 nuclei acquire a proton and two neutrons, producing small amounts of the isotope of the third lightest element, lithium. While the temperature is still high enough for nuclear fusion, the continuing expansion will drive the nuclei, protons, and neutrons too far apart to produce any more elements.

2 HELIUM-3

The addition of another proton makes helium-3, which consists of two protons and a neutron. A very small amount of the helium still remains in this form. Helium-3 and the more common helium-4 are *isotopes* of helium, with the same number of protons but a different number of neutrons.

Helium-4

Mopping up the neutrons

The creation of the elements (nucleosynthesis) had the effect of mopping up all the neutrons and tying them up in nuclei, almost entirely helium. This also stabilized the neutrons, preventing them from decaying into protons. Some of the protons also ended up in nuclei, but they were so numerous that most protons remained free – as hydrogen nuclei. As a result, the Universe should have ended up with ten times more hydrogen than helium. Put another way, helium – which is heavier than hydrogen – should make up about a quarter of the mass of the Universe today.

3 HELIUM-4

A final neutron arrives to create a nucleus of helium-4, the most common variety of the second lightest element. Most of this helium has survived billions of years and is still around today. When you buy a party balloon that floats in air, it is filled with helium gas created when the Universe was only three minutes old!

Sifting through the ashes

The "ashes" of the Big Bang – the elements created in its first three minutes – should work out to be 77% hydrogen, 23% helium, and 0.000,000,1% lithium, according to detailed calculations. How can we check if the composition of the cosmos matches up? Our part of the Galaxy has suffered "pollution" by elements produced more recently in stars. But some gas clouds far out in space consist of material virtually unaltered since the Big Bang. By analyzing the light from these gas clouds, or nebulae, astronomers can find exactly how much of each element they contain. The answer is that there are tiny amounts of lithium, while hydrogen and helium come in at 77% and 23% – powerful evidence for the Big Bang.

The Orion Nebula is a glowing cloud of hydrogen and helium in which stars have just been born.

Echoes of the Big Bang

AFTER ITS BUSY FIRST THREE MINUTES, when particles came and went and the first elements were forged, the Universe settled down in a much calmer period that lasted more than a quarter of a million years. The ingredients of the cosmos stayed the same, merely becoming ever more dilute as the Universe continued to expand. The main component was radiation, continually bouncing off the particles of matter to form an impenetrable luminous fog. But one day, the fog abruptly cleared. The echoes of that momentous event still survive as a background of heat radiation filling the Universe. It is powerful evidence that the Big Bang really did happen.

Universe clears

Three hundred thousand years after the Big Bang, the Universe suddenly changed from being an opaque fireball to being the clear, transparent cosmos we live in today. The key to the change was heat – or rather, the lack of heat in the expanding and ever-cooling Universe. Once the temperature had dropped to about 5,500°F (3,000°C) – about half the temperature of the Sun's surface – matter formed itself into atoms, which allow radiation to pass unhindered.

The darker regions are where dark matter is beginning to clump together.

DOMINATED BY RADIATION

A slice through the early Universe reveals a uniform fog of radiation. At first it was mainly in the form of energetic gamma rays; as the cosmos cooled it changed to X-rays and, ultimately, light and heat (infrared radiation). Because the radiation kept the electrons apart from the protons and helium nuclei, this is called the "radiation-dominated era." Dark matter, in the form of WIMPs and/or neutrinos, was unaffected by radiation and began to clump together thanks to gravity.

THE FOGGY, FOGGY UNIVERSE

Seen on the smallest scales, the hot, early Universe was a seething pot-pourri of dark matter, radiation, atomic nuclei, and electrons. In particular, the electrons and photons were constantly in battle with each other. Photons and electrons parried continuously, and neither got anywhere. Photons would bounce off one electron, only to collide with another, then another. Because light is carried by photons, light could never travel in a straight line – and as a result, the Universe was opaque.

Hydrogen nucleus: a single proton

Electron

Helium nucleus: two protons and two neutrons

Photons cannot travel in straight lines, so you would not be able to see more than a fraction of a millimeter.

The "last scattering surface" – the "wall" dividing the opaque from the transparent Universe

Photons and electrons were constantly colliding in the high temperatures left after the Big Bang. For 300,000 years, the Universe was foggy.

SUDDEN CLEARING

As the Universe cooled, the electrons moved more slowly and found it more and more difficult to resist being attracted to the positive electric charge of the protons and other nuclei. When the temperature dropped to 5,500°F (3,000°C), they were pulled into orbit around the nuclei to form the first atoms of hydrogen, helium, and lithium. Once the electrons were locked up in atoms, they lost the freedom to hinder the passing photons. Light had a free passage – and space became transparent.

The first atoms form: hydrogen (one proton and one electron) and helium (two protons, two neutrons, and two electrons).

Light (blue wiggly line) is not affected by the bound electrons, and travels unimpeded through the Universe.

After the clearing, the "matter-dominated" era begins – and has continued to the present day. Clumps of dark matter start to attract the hydrogen-helium gas around them, forming huge clouds that will eventually become galaxies.

Radiation from the "last scattering surface" travels far into the future. As the Universe expands, the radiation cools down, changing from heat and light to radio waves.

FINDING THE AFTERGLOW

In the early 1960s, physicists Arno Penzias and Robert Wilson started to search for faint radio signals, called microwaves, from the outskirts of our Galaxy. For this, they chose a particularly sensitive radio telescope, a 20-ft (6-meter) horn antenna at Holmdel, New Jersey. But it seemed to be bedeviled with interference – a constant signal from all over the sky, corresponding to radiation at a temperature of −454°F (−270°C or 3 degrees above absolute zero). They thought the signal arose from pigeon droppings in the telescope, but colleagues realized that this "microwave background" was the hot afterglow of the Big Bang, now cooled down by the expansion of the Universe. It was the clinching evidence that the Universe began in a hot Big Bang.

Penzias and Wilson next to the antenna with which they discovered the background of heat radiation.

THE SAME IN ALL DIRECTIONS

Wherever you are on Earth you look outward into space and backward in time. That's because all radiation including light and radio waves, takes time to reach you. Look a short distance into space, and you are surrounded by nearby stars a few light-years away. A larger telescope picks out galaxies as they were millions of years ago, and a larger one still can detect quasars billions of years ago. The most distant radiation a telescope can detect comes from the "last scattering surface" – the "wall" where the heat radiation escapes from the early fog. Whatever direction it points, the telescope can see back in time to this "wall." As a result, the background of heat radiation comes to us with equal intensity from all directions.

The "wall"
Quasars
Far galaxies
Nearest galaxies
Nearby stars

Earth   *Nearby stars*   *Nearest galaxies*   *Far galaxies*   *Quasars*   *The "wall"*

When we detect the microwave background, we are looking back to 300,000 years after the Big Bang. We cannot see any farther back, because before then the Universe was opaque.

Ripples in space

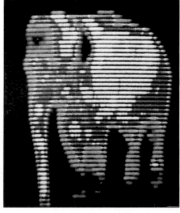

A "heat image" shows which parts of an elephant are a few degrees hotter or colder. COBE measured differences a million times smaller.

A FTER THE COSMIC FOG CLEARED, at an age of 300,000 years, the stage was set for a major change. Radiation was still around in vast abundance, but it was no longer boss. Matter now started to control its own fate, under the ruling force of its own gravity. Atoms of hydrogen and helium pulled on each other, and both felt the gravitational pull of the dark matter (WIMPs and/or neutrinos). Over hundreds of millions of years, the gas coagulated into clouds, like milk curdling into cheese. Our evidence for these events is a faint pattern of ripples in the background heat radiation.

The Cosmic Background Explorer (COBE) carried three telescopes tuned in to heat radiation left over from the Big Bang.

Cosmic thermometer

If the matter in the early, expanding Universe had been the same temperature and density everywhere, the gas would have spread out ever more thinly, and the Universe today would consist of only rarefied gas. In fact, it contains galaxies, stars, and planets. The seeds of these clumps of matter must have been sown in the original dense fog, imprinting a pattern of cooler patches in the heat radiation from this era. From the mid-1960s, astronomers searched in vain for these elusive ripples. Success came in 1992, with the COBE satellite. It was the world's most sensitive thermometer, built to probe the chill temperatures of deep space.

HEAT OF THE NIGHT

In COBE's heat image of the entire sky, the colored ripples reveal regions that are just a few millionths of a degree hotter (pink) or colder (blue) than average. The denser patches appear blue because the radiation cools as it escapes from the greater gravitational pull.

Denser regions of gas (blue in COBE's map) pull together because of their own gravity. In between, low density (pink) regions expand to become empty voids.

The gases detected by COBE lie so far away that they show the Universe as it was almost 13 billion years ago, just 300,000 years after the Big Bang.

The warm and cooler ripples show how gas from the original fireball was starting to break up into denser patches.

Expanding picture

This is the story of one region of the Universe, from its portrait in the COBE map through to the clumps of gas forming long strings, known as filaments, that would condense into the first galaxies. Between lie vast voids of empty space, some more than a hundred million light-years across.

GROWING VOIDS AND FILAMENTS

The Universe 300 million years after the Big Bang resembled a piece of Swiss cheese. Clusters of galaxies had formed from the denser clumps of gas. They lay in long filaments surrounding empty voids. Where filaments met, the galaxies swarm in denser congregations, called superclusters. From this point, the Universe simply expanded, giving rise to the distribution of galaxies we observe today.

COBE has revealed why galaxies today are spread out as filaments surrounding voids.

The longest filaments are called "walls" of galaxies.

The voids contain few galaxies.

Some astronomers think the gas clouds were marshaled into filaments by the gravity of cosmic strings surviving from the earliest moments of the Universe.

The dots show the distribution of hydrogen and helium gases starting to turn into galaxies.

WHERE IS THE DARK MATTER TODAY?

Astronomers do not know how the dark matter is spread now. It could be clumped together with the galaxies, or spread more evenly between the filaments and voids.

The route to galaxy birth

Two competing theories describe how COBE's "curdled" lumps of gas came to form galaxies grouped into clusters and super-clusters. In each case, the basic ingredients are the hydrogen and helium gases from the Big Bang, condensing under the gravitational influence of the dark matter. If most of the dark matter consists of neutrinos, it leads to the "top down" theory of galaxy formation; if WIMPs predominate, we get the "bottom up" version of events.

TOP DOWN THEORY

According to the "top down" theory, huge filaments of gas split into smaller clouds, which then split again. The filaments define the size and shape of the final superclusters and clusters well before each small gas cloud turns into an individual galaxy.

BOTTOM UP THEORY

According to the "bottom up" theory, huge numbers of galaxies were born very soon after the period seen by COBE. At first these galaxies were scattered randomly, but gravity then pulled them together to make clusters and superclusters.

SEARCHING FOR SMALLER RIPPLES

These miniature radio telescopes in the Canary Islands are looking for smaller ripples than COBE detected to discover more precisely how galaxies, including our own Milky Way, were born from the cosmic fireball. Along with other sensitive telescopes at locations ranging from Antarctica to high-flying balloons, the radio horns are designed to discover ripples small enough to have been the seeds of galaxies.

Birth of the Milky Way

ASTRONOMERS CAN DATE WHEN THE BIG BANG TOOK PLACE, but can only guess that the galaxies formed about half a billion years later. Their instruments cannot record the subtle coming together of gas clouds that resulted in the creation of billions of galaxies. Fortunately, youthful galaxies undergo violent outbursts that can be witnessed halfway across the Universe – but after that, they settle down. And that's lucky for us since we live in such a galaxy. This is the story of our Milky Way from its own birth to the day it created the Sun and planets.

Our Galaxy is born as countless warm gas clouds come together under the pull of gravity. Stars are born as clouds collide.

A great deal of gas starts to accumulate in the galaxy's core. Its gravity becomes so great that a massive black hole forms and grows.

Gas and stars spiral into the black hole, forming a superhot whirlpool called an accretion disk. This brilliant disk is a quasar.

Cross-section of the quasar's accretion disk and its high-speed jets

The jets from a radio galaxy billow out into huge clouds.

A violent youth

In its youth, the center of our Galaxy probably flared into life as a quasar. A quasar is the tiny, dazzling core of a very young and active galaxy. At its heart is a supermassive black hole, voraciously gobbling gas – and shooting what it doesn't eat far out into space. Astronomers have found thousands of quasars, most so remote they look like very faint stars.

A quasar sends out two jets of charged particles at almost the speed of light.

The quasar has evolved into a radio galaxy.

A CHANGING UNIVERSE

When astronomers look out to great distances, they are looking back in time to the Universe as it was in its youth. They find that many more distant galaxies have quasars at their core than nearby galaxies. So the Universe is changing with time, as the Big Bang theory predicts. This rules out theories that suggest the Universe is infinitely old and unchanging.

Quasar

The early Universe (small sphere) contains many more quasars and radio galaxies than the Universe of today (large sphere).

MARTIN RYLE

In the late 1950s, the British astronomer Martin Ryle (1918-1984) used a radio telescope that he and his team had built at Cambridge to look at galaxies in the distant Universe. He came up with the first evidence that galaxies were more tightly packed together in the past and that the young Universe was dominated by quasars.

GROWING LESS VIOLENT

Our Galaxy's quasar phase lasted for only a few million years. Next it embarked on a less violent phase as a radio galaxy. The jets it beamed out as a quasar billowed out into two enormous clouds generating powerful radio waves. There was still potential for outbursts from the core – the black hole was there, lurking – but as gas was used up to make stars, the black hole was slowly starved.

The radio-emitting jets can span more than a million light-years.

SETTLING DOWN

Nine billion years after its fiery birth, our Milky Way was starting to settle down. A huge black hole, weighing in at three million star masses, still lurked at its core; but it was quiescent, for gas fodder was not as plentiful as before. The Galaxy had by now given birth to billions of stars, arranged in a beautiful spiral shape 100,000 light-years across. But there was always room for more.

Pillars of starbirth: young stars emerging from a pillar of dust and gas in the Eagle Nebula about 7,000 years ago

A STAR IS BORN

Some 4.6 billion years ago, a cloud of dust and gas started to collapse in an anonymous suburb of the Milky Way. As it shrank, it spun faster, eventually becoming a disk. At its heart, it grew hotter and denser, until the core flashed into life. A star, our Sun, had been born. Powered by nuclear fusion reactions, the young Sun showered light and energy onto its emerging family: the nine planets forming in the surrounding disk.

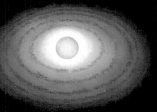

The young Sun forms in a disk of gas and dust.

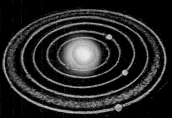

The surrounding disk condenses into the planets, including Earth.

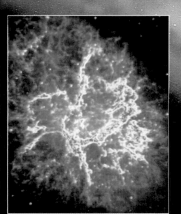

Crab Nebula: the remains of a dying star that blasted heavy elements across space

STARTING WITH HYDROGEN...

All stars can combine the nuclei of hydrogen in their cores to make helium, a reaction that gives out energy. The heavier stars can also fuse three heliums to create carbon.

The heavy gang

George Gamow believed that all the elements were created in the Big Bang. But now we know that it made only the lightest – hydrogen, helium, and lithium. It turns out that the other 89 elements, making up just 1% of the total material in the Universe, were forged in the nuclear furnaces of stars. They were then scattered throughout space by stars shedding matter in their death throes.

...ENDING WITH IRON

Massive stars can create elements as heavy as iron in their cores. When they try to fuse iron, they explode as supernovas, blasting their outer layers into space. In the fury of the explosion, even heavier elements can be synthesized.

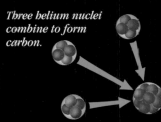

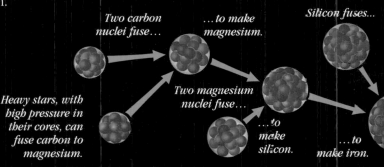

Three helium nuclei combine to form carbon.

Each helium nucleus consists of two protons and two neutrons.

Heavy stars, with high pressure in their cores, can fuse carbon to magnesium.

Two carbon nuclei fuse...

...to make magnesium.

Two magnesium nuclei fuse...

...to make silicon.

Silicon fuses...

...to make iron.

The heaviest stars can fuse two nuclei of silicon to make iron.

...UP

...mmediately after
... the busiest ever.
...ture soared, and
...rgy surge fueled
... of particle and
...creation. Many
...icles came into
... with oddities
...ature black holes
...trings. This
... trillion trillion
...on trillion trillion
... than water.

CREATION OF MATTER
The massed forces of particles now started to fight. Closely matched armies of matter and antimatter annihilated each other in floods of radiation. Intense radiation all around created reinforcements in the form of new matter-antimatter pairs. But in the end, radiation weakened too much to create new pairs, and the slight surplus of matter won out.

FIRST ELEMENTS
Although the young Universe was still a frenzy of activity, it was cooling fast. This meant that it could now embark on feats of construction. By the end of its third minute, it had succeeded in welding protons and neutrons into the nuclei of the first elements — hydrogen, helium, and a smattering of lithium. The density was now 10 times that of water.

ECHOES OF THE BIG BANG
After the hurly-burly of its extreme youth, the Universe relaxed. At the age of 20 minutes, the density dropped below that of water. The foggy, opaque mass continued to expand and cool. Then, 300,000 years after its birth, it became transparent. Looking back to that instant, sensitive radio telescopes can see the divide — the opaque wall of the dying fireball of the Big Bang.

10^{-4}	10^0	10^4	10^8	10^{12}
0.0001 second	1 second	3 hours	3 years	30,000 year

The underground particle accelerator (outlined here in yellow) at CERN, near Geneva, Switerland, can "see" farther than any telescope. It recreates the conditions in the Big Bang by smashing particles violently together.

...UP

... included the
...uarks and leptons
...mong the massive
...sons, Higgs bosons,
...c monopoles.
...rticles – gluons,
...nd Z bosons, and
...lso abounded.

CREATION OF MATTER
By the end of the era, the building blocks — protons, neutrons, electrons, and neutrinos — were in place. The density had dropped to a million times that of water.

FIRST ELEMENTS
To begin with, protons and neutrons were around in equal numbers. But neutrons are unstable, and decay into protons — so protons gained the upper hand. This is reflected in the proportions of the early elements created: 77% hydrogen to 23% helium.

ECHOES OF THE BIG BANG
Inside the fog, the Universe was busy. Invisible dark matter was gathering into the beginnings of galaxies. When the temperature dropped to 5,500°F (3,000°C), electrons suddenly combined with nuclei to make atoms. Light, until then obstructed by electrons, had free passage — so the Universe cleared.

...t Big Bang, the Universe has been cooling. At inflation,
...osive that its temperature dropped to almost zero. But
...nflation flooded the Universe with energy, and the
temperature shot up again. Unless the Universe is
closed, it will continue steadily cooling.

10^{-4}	10^0	10^4	Time (seconds)	10^8	10^{12}

Unfolding Universe

HERE IS A TRULY BRIEF history of time. These four pages cover the entire story of our Universe, from creation to doomsday. New technologies, telescopes, and advances in particle physics have all played their part in unraveling the mystery. But there are still huge blanks to fill in. Thanks to particle accelerators on Earth, we know more about the first few seconds of the Universe than about the following half billion years. And no matter how much we try to extrapolate from present knowledge, what happens in the future will always involve some crystal-ball gazing.

Past, present, and future

This foldout of the Universe's past and future begins with the Big Bang. Time also starts with the Big Bang and flows from left to right. In order to fit everything in, the timescale is compressed more and more as time goes on. Each section corresponds to a spread in the book, and is divided into two halves. Along the top, we see how the Universe evolves on the grand scale; below, we find out what the particles are up to (for a key to the particles, see pages 14-15). The foldout finishes with two possible ends for the Universe: the Big Crunch, or expansion forever.

FATHER OF THE BIG BANG

In 1917, Albert Einstein proposed a description of the Universe based on his new theory of general relativity. It inspired many other theorists, including Willem de Sitter in Holland and Alexandr Friedmann in Russia. In Belgium, Georges Lemaître (1894-1966) came up with his own model when he heard that the Universe was expanding. He made an intellectual leap by suggesting that the Universe began as a "primeval atom" — something hot and dense that had exploded, causing space to expand. Although today's theories include new ideas, such as inflation, Lemaître can truly be called the father of the Big Bang.

Georges Lemaître was ordained as a priest before studying cosmology.

T EQUALS ZERO

The Big Bang was the beginning of both space and time. It came out of nowhere: an almost infinitely hot fireball that started expanding as soon as it appeared. There was no "before" the Big Bang, for time only started when creation took place.

T EQUALS ZERO

The young Universe was a seething cauldron of radiation. Its energy was so enormous that matter and antimatter appeared spontaneously, but were quickly annihilated again in a burst of energy that kept the fires stoked up.

BLOWUP

Although we call the instant of creation the Big Bang, many astronomers believe it was a fairly small one — equivalent to exploding a bag of sugar. They suggest that fractions of a second after "ignition," the Universe literally blew up. In this period of cosmic inflation, it increased its size a hundred trillion trillion trillion trillion times. Inflation explains why the Universe is so big and so uniform today.

BLOWUP

If this theory is correct, inflation made nearly all the mass there is in the Universe. It flooded the Universe with energy, turning virtual particles into real matter.

PARTICLE SO

The period i inflation wa The tempera the huge en an explosion antiparticle massive part being, along such as min and cosmic "soup" was trillion trilli times denser

PARTICLE SO

The particle lightweight swimming a WIMPs, X bo and magnet Messenger p photons, W gravitons —

A COOLING UNIVERSE

Since the almost infinitely ho its growth was so ex the end of

Temperature (degrees)

10^{28} 10^{26} 10^{24} 10^{22} 10^{20} 10^{16} 10^{12} 10^{8} 10^{4} 0

0 10^{-36} 10^{-32} 10^{-28} 10^{-24} 10^{-20} 10^{-16} 10^{-12} 10^{-8}

10^{-32} 10^{-36} 10^{-28} 10^{-24} 10^{-20} 10^{-16} 10^{-12} 10^{-8}

trillion-trillionth second   trillionth second   0.0 sec

Creation myths

WHEN THE UNIVERSE reached 9 billion years, a small and undistinguished planet was born. At first, it was a hot, violent world, but as it cooled, life somehow arose and gained a stronghold. First plants, then animals, and finally humans appeared on the scene. They exploded into scores of different cultures. But common to each were the questions "Where did we come from?" and "How did it all begin?" The first ideas on creation ranged from the wildly romantic Aztec myths to the pragmatic Judeo-Christian approach.

EVOLUTION OF EARTH
Earth was born from millions of rocky fragments formed from tiny particles of dust around the young Sun. More rocky fragments, meteorites, bombarded the surface, heating it until it glowed. As the hot and molten surface cooled, water vapor condensed as clouds and then filled the oceans. The thin surface crust of rock split into continents, pushed around by currents of molten rock within the planet.

Meteorite impacts blast its surface.

Earth forms from cloud of dust and gas.

Clouds cloak Earth, later condensing as rain, which creates oceans in low-lying regions.

The single landmass, known as Pangea, starts to break up as internal heat currents break the crust apart.

Seven days of creation
Judeo-Christians believe that "In the beginning, God created the Heaven and the Earth." Over the next six days, God worked hard on his creation: establishing day and night, oceans, land, and plants by day three; the stars, Sun and Moon, sea creatures, and birds by day five. On the sixth day, he made animals and the pinnacle of his creation, humans. He set aside the seventh day for rest – which is why Sunday is holy to Christians.

God, having created Heaven and Earth, marvels at his handiwork.

Atum has spoken
The ancient Egyptians, whose civilization lasted for more than two millennia, wove many intricate myths. They believed that the Universe began when the god Atum came into being, simply by calling his own name. Next, Atum vomited up his brother and sister, Shu and Tefnut, who in turn gave birth to the god Geb (who symbolized the Earth) and the goddess Nut (the sky). All the people of Egypt were descended from the children of Nut and Geb. The whole act of creation was watched over by the all-seeing, non-interfering Eye.

In Egyptian mythology, the lovers Geb (the Earth) and Nut (the sky) are separated from one another so that day can take place. At night they are reunited.

THEORY REPLACES MYTH
In the 20th century, discoveries of the expanding Universe, a background of heat radiation, and the amount of hydrogen and helium in the cosmos have given us a theory – not a myth – of the origin of the Universe, as summarized on the foldout pages underneath this page. But we may never know *why* the Universe began.

Cosmic egg

The Chinese Universe began with a huge cosmic egg containing *yin-yang*. This comprised everything and its exact opposite: male-female, cold-heat, dark-light. Within the *yin-yang* was the god Phan Ku: his eyes became the Sun and Moon; his breath the wind; his hair the trees and plants; his flesh the Earth; his sweat rain; and eventually the worms that left his rotting body turned into people.

In another version of the Chinese creation myth Pan-Kou-Che, the Creator, chips away at his great work among the swirling clouds.

Quetzalcoatl and Tezcatlipoca

The Aztecs of Mexico had many creation legends. One concerns the gods Quetzalcoatl and Tezcatlipoca, who pulled the goddess Coatlicue down from the heavens and ripped her in two – creating the sky and the Earth. Her body became mountains and valleys; her hair turned into plants. But Coatlicue was unhappy at her treatment and demanded frequent sacrifices of human hearts.

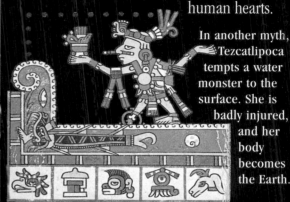

In another myth, Tezcatlipoca tempts a water monster to the surface. She is badly injured, and her body becomes the Earth.

Prajapati and the golden egg

Several of the creation myths in the Hindu culture feature gods coming into being by uttering their names. Others describe great oceans, and a few involve cosmic eggs. One such legend concerns an ocean that gave birth to a golden egg. After a year, Prajapati emerged from the egg. He rested on the shell for another year before trying to speak. The first sound he made became the Earth; the second, the sky; and the third, the seasons.

Vishnu, one of the Hindu gods associated with creation

Earth's continents today are still on the move, driven by currents of rock deep below. Their separation has led to forms of life and human cultures that are unique to each continent.

Aboriginal Dreamtime

Central to the Australian Aboriginal culture is "Dreamtime": an era when ancestors went on journeys, creating "dreamings" that became people, sacred sites, and traditions. The ancestors were often lizards; warmed by the Sun, they became human. The god of the Dieri Aboriginals made the first human in the form of a lizard, but found it could walk only when its tail had been cut off. The Dreamtime ancestors are celebrated in dramatic rock paintings.

Dreamtime: two of the Aboriginals' magical flying ancestors, who created sacred sites and creatures where they touched down.

FAR FUTURE (OPEN)

An open Universe will expand forever. In each galaxy, the star corpses will either fall into the central black hole or be whirled out into space. They will eventually decay into radiation, while the supermassive black holes will explode. Nothing larger than subatomic particles will remain.

DARK MATTER IN CONTROL

For more than 50 years, astronomers have suspected that there is far more matter in the Universe than they can see in the form of stars, gas, and galaxies. Although this "dark matter" is invisible, its gravity pulls on the ordinary matter and will ultimately determine the fate of the expanding Universe. Astronomers are uncertain how much dark matter there is. Measurements of galaxies (see below) show that dark matter makes up at least 90% of the Universe. The theory of inflation puts it at 99%: an amount that means the Universe is always on the brink between perpetual expansion and ultimate collapse.

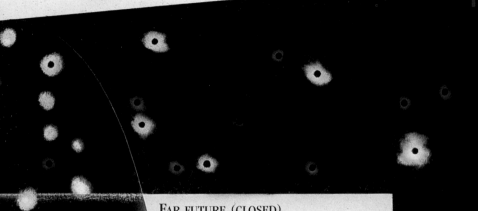

FAR FUTURE (CLOSED)

A closed Universe, which contains enough dark matter to exert sufficient gravitational "brakes," will expand, reach a limit, and then shrink back. Rather than death by cold, it will be death by fire as the Universe races to oblivion in a Big Crunch. In this time-reversal of the Big Bang, space will disappear and time will come to a halt, in ultimate oblivion.

From a viewpoint in the far future of an infinitely old Universe, the period of time that has elapsed from the Big Bang to now (including our existence) will seem like the blink of an eye.

10^{20}

3 trillion years

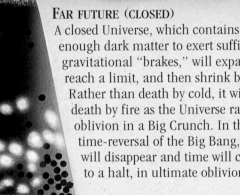

FAR FUTURE (CLOSED)

At first, stars live out their lives as they do in an open Universe. But about 3 million years before the Big Crunch, galaxies — now supermassive black holes — start to merge. As the collapse proceeds, the temperature of the background radiation climbs to that of the stars. With three minutes to go, the black holes merge; then it's Crunch time.

WEIGHING UP THE EVIDENCE

The extra gravity of dark matter — outweighing ordinary matter ten times over — is needed to keep whirling galaxies together and to rein in the speeding galaxies into clusters. Much more may lurk in the space between. Some dark matter may be failed stars, but most probably consists of WIMPs and/or neutrinos.

FAR FUTURE (OPEN)

An ever-expanding open Universe will become darker and emptier as stars die, matter decays, and black holes explode. At the very end, the tiny particles born in the Big Bang will have the last say. The infinite future will be one of a bitterly cold expanse, thinly populated with electrons, positrons, neutrinos, and the elusive WIMPs.

...timescale is marked in ...conds, shown as powers of ten ...e Glossary), and also in more ...iliar units such as trillionths ...t second, hours, and years.

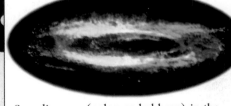

Speeding gas (color-coded here) in the Andromeda Galaxy is in the gravitational grip of dark matter filling the galaxy.

RIPPLES IN SPACE

As the cosmic fog cleared, matter was "curdling," like milk turning into cheese, imprinting distinctive "ripples" in the radiation background. Freed from the domination of radiation, matter was in charge of its own destiny. It heralded a new era in the cosmos: huge structures, in the form of galaxies, could start to emerge.

BIRTH OF THE MILKY WAY

Many galaxies had violent youths, going through quasar outbursts before settling down to become placid star cities. In a quiet suburb of one such galaxy, an ordinary star was born 4.6 billion years ago. But it was special to us: the Sun, with its planets, had come into existence.

NEAR FUTURE

The stars' days are numbered. In 5 billion years, our Sun will use up all its fuel and end its days a white dwarf. Bigger stars will end up as neutron stars, or even black holes. Galaxies will become graveyards of star corpses orbiting supermassive black holes.

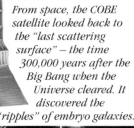
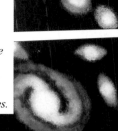
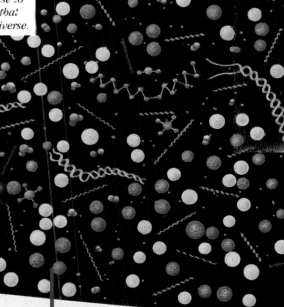

The Hubble Space Telescope was designed to study the era of galaxy formation, about half a billion years after the Big Bang. It has found many young galaxies, some apparently newly born.

From space, the COBE satellite looked back to the "last scattering surface" – the time 300,000 years after the Big Bang when the Universe cleared. It discovered the "ripples" of embryo galaxies.

Today the Universe is in its prime – although youth is still on its side. Abundant raw material remains to make new stars.

10^{16}	$10^{17.5}$	10
300 million years	*13 billion years*	*1*

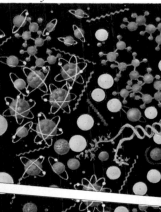

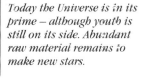

By now, atoms have built up molecules so complex that they have given rise to living things: entities that can ponder on the Universe.

RIPPLES IN SPACE

As radiation whistled powerlessly by, the particles of matter flexed their gravitational muscles on each other. Dark matter led the way, marshaling the atoms of hydrogen, helium, and lithium into dense clumps: the seeds of our own existence.

BIRTH OF THE MILKY WAY

Stars picked up the baton of element creation from the Big Bang. Deep in their cores, they forged helium from hydrogen, carbon from helium, and beyond. These elements became the basis of life.

NEAR FUTURE

Hydrogen gas, the raw material of starbirth, begins to run out. Only heavier atoms remain, which cannot fuel stars. And tiny black holes, created in the Big Bang, are exploding. They vanish in puffs of radiation.

The se (s. fam of

Present day
10^{16}
$10^{17.5}$

Scale of space

BEFORE PEOPLE COULD UNDERSTAND the history of the Universe, they had to figure out its geography. But plumbing the depths of space was not easy: objects in the sky looked as if they were all at the same distance, pinned to the great dome of the sky. Fortunately, the Moon and planets gave away their relative closeness by virtue of their movement. By the 17th century, astronomers realized that the Sun was the center of the Solar System and they began to measure the distances to planets. Two centuries later, they extended the tape measure to the nearest stars, almost a million times farther away. Early in the 20th century, they identified individual stars in distant galaxies and could extend the ladder of cosmic distances more than a million times farther.

PARALLAX WORKS FOR UP TO 300 LIGHT-YEARS
A nearby object appears to shift against a distant background when viewed from two positions – that's the principle behind parallax. If you know the length of the "baseline" between the two positions, and can measure the shift, it is simple geometry to calculate the object's distance. This method works for stars up to 300 light-years away.

Earth's position in December

In parallax measurements, the baseline is the diameter of Earth's orbit, equal to 2 AU.

Earth's position in Jun

Scale of the Universe

From planets to the remotest galaxies, astronomers can measure the distance to any object. They use a "ladder" of methods – planetary speeds, parallax, Cepheid stars, and whole galaxies. Each depends on the previous step, so distances grow increasingly uncertain: the farthest galaxies may be 30 percent nearer or farther than estimated.

PTOLEMAIC THEORY
The ancient Greeks believed that the Sun, Moon, and planets circled the Earth. To explain the fact that planets sometimes travel backward in the sky, the Greeks thought each moved in a small circle (an epicycle) that was itself orbiting Earth. Ptolemy summarized the theory in the *Almagest*, written in the 2nd century AD.

COPERNICAN THEORY
The Ptolemaic theory held sway until 1543, when the Polish monk Nicolaus Copernicus suggested that the Sun lay at the center of things. The Church, however, taught that the Earth was central: his theory was heresy. Perhaps this is why he did not publish it until the day he died.

The edge of the Milky Way lies 50,000 ly away. This "non-linear" scale makes the stars seem more crowded at the edge. Viewed normally, the center of the Galaxy is the most dense.

Beta Centauri
460 ly

100 ly

WITHIN THE SOLAR SYSTEM
Astronomers find the distance to planets from the speed they orbit the Sun. Those nearest the Sun move fastest to avoid being pulled in by its gravity. Mercury, 36 million miles (58 million km) from the Sun, speeds around at 30 miles/sec (48 km/sec). Pluto, almost a hundred times farther out, travels at a leisurely 2.9 miles/sec (4.7 km/sec). The Earth's distance from the Sun – the astronomical unit (AU) – is the first step in a long ladder of distances.

Alpha and Beta Centauri appear to be of similar brightness in the sky, but brilliant Beta is 100 times farther away.

Alpha Centauri
4.3 ly

Earth

Pluto
49.3 AU

1 ly

Earth to Sun is 92.95 million miles (149.6 million km), or 1 AU.

LIGHT-YEARS AWAY
Astronomers describe the huge distances to the stars in terms of light-years. Light moves at 186,000 miles/sec (300,000 km/sec), and in a year it travels 5.9 trillion miles (9.5 trillion km), or 1 light-year (ly). It equals 63,240 AU. The nearest star, Alpha Centauri, is 25 trillion miles (40 trillion km) away – 4.3 ly. Most of the stars we can see with the naked eye in the sky are within 1,000 ly.

Extragalactic distances

Most galaxies lie millions of light-years away. Astronomers measure their distances by comparing the apparent brightness of their most luminous stars, the supergiants, with supergiants in our own Galaxy. For more remote galaxies, they compare the brightness of globular star clusters – or the whole galaxy – with nearby examples. Distances to the farthest clusters of galaxies are estimated by measuring the apparent brightness of their biggest members.

The Coma Cluster is a cluster of 5,000 or more galaxies lying 300 million ly away. It lies at the center of a supercluster containing millions of galaxies.

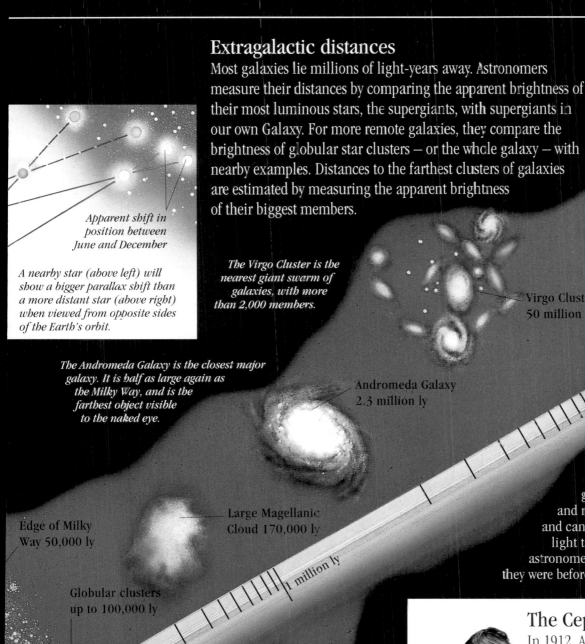

Apparent shift in position between June and December

A nearby star (above left) will show a bigger parallax shift than a more distant star (above right) when viewed from opposite sides of the Earth's orbit.

The Virgo Cluster is the nearest giant swarm of galaxies, with more than 2,000 members.

Virgo Cluster
50 million ly

The Andromeda Galaxy is the closest major galaxy. It is half as large again as the Milky Way, and is the farthest object visible to the naked eye.

Andromeda Galaxy
2.3 million ly

100 million ly

MORE DISTANT SHORES

Astronomers can measure distances to clusters of galaxies billions of light-years away. Many galaxies in clusters are much bigger and more luminous than our Milky Way, and can be seen at these vast distances. The light takes so long to reach the Earth that astronomers are seeing the farthest clusters as they were before the Sun and its planets were born.

Edge of Milky
Way 50,000 ly

Large Magellanic
Cloud 170,000 ly

Globular clusters
up to 100,000 ly

1 million ly

Small Magellanic
Cloud 190,000 ly

The Large and Small Magellanic Clouds are the closest galaxies to us. They orbit the Milky Way and are visible to the naked eye.

10,000 ly

The Cepheid yardstick

In 1912, American astronomer Henrietta Leavitt (1868-1921) was studying Cepheid variables – stars that oscillate in brightness in regular cycles – in the Small Magellanic Cloud. She discovered that the length of the cycle revealed a Cepheid's true brightness. Hence they are standard candles, which can be used to measure the distances to other galaxies containing Cepheids.

Henrietta Leavitt worked at the Harvard College Observatory.

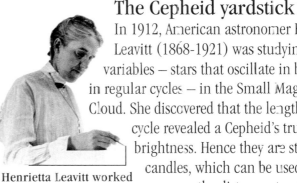

The Cepheid cycle

Shrinking and dimmest

Expanding and brightest

Largest

Smallest

STANDARD CANDLES

If two stars are putting out the same amount of light, but one appears a hundred times dimmer, it must lie ten times farther away. In reality, stars have different luminosities, but astronomers have identified stars such as Cepheids and supergiants that shine with the same brightness. The brightness of the globular clusters of stars surrounding galaxies can also be used as standard candles.

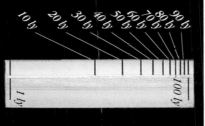

10 ly 20 ly 30 ly 40 ly 50 ly 60 ly 70 ly 80 ly 90 ly

1 ly   100 ly

COSMIC TAPE MEASURE

The Universe is so vast that it is difficult to represent on a page. Here, we have used a non-linear scale that is increasingly compressed: each major division is 100 times more compressed than the previous one.

WHY CEPHEIDS ARE IMPORTANT

Cepheids are thousands of times brighter than the Sun and this, coupled with their cycle of brightening and dimming, makes them easy to recognize in distant galaxies. An astronomer finds the true brightness of a Cepheid from the time it takes to change from bright to dim and back to bright. Comparing that star's apparent with its true brightness gives the distance to its parent galaxy.

Galaxies on the move

TWO BREAKTHROUGHS IN OUR UNDERSTANDING of the Universe came in the 1920s thanks to American astronomer Edwin Hubble. For centuries, astronomers believed the Milky Way comprised the entire Universe. Hubble was among the first to realize that some of the fuzzy patches, or "nebulae," in the sky were galaxies far beyond our own. His second breakthrough came in 1929. By spreading out the light from each galaxy into a spectrum, he could determine what it was made of and how fast it was moving. To his surprise, most of the galaxies were moving away from ours. There was nothing repulsive about our Galaxy: it was just that the Universe itself was expanding.

When a galaxy is receding, its light waves are stretched. The spectral lines move toward longer, redder wavelengths, and you measure a redshift.

When you spread light from a stationary galaxy into a spectrum, you see dark bands (spectral lines) at particular wavelengths.

When a galaxy approaches you, its light waves are compressed. Its spectral lines move toward shorter, bluer wavelengths and you measure a blueshift.

COSMIC SPEEDOMETER
If sound or light waves are radiating from a moving object, the waves in front become bunched together, while those behind trail. This is the Doppler effect, familiar to everyone who has heard the high pitch of an ambulance siren approaching, and the lower pitch of it receding. The faster it goes, the bigger the change in pitch.

Expanding Universe

The vast majority of galaxies, with the exception of a few nearby ones such as Andromeda, are moving away from us. The galaxies themselves are not moving, it is the space between them that stretches as the Universe expands. In these successive snapshots of the expanding Universe, we see the light from three other galaxies traveling to reach the Milky Way. The more distant the galaxy, the more expanding space lies between the galaxy and us, so the faster it is moving. The higher speed produces a larger redshift in the galaxy's light.

EXPANSIVE ASTRONOMER
Edwin Hubble qualified as a brilliant lawyer before turning to astronomy. His outstanding astronomical contributions were made at the Mount Wilson telescope overlooking Los Angeles in California, often in collaboration with Milton Humason — a former mule driver up to the mountaintop telescope.

Edwin Hubble (1889-1953) in whose honor the Hubble Space Telescope is named.

3 PRESENT
Because the most distant galaxy is moving fastest, its light shows the biggest redshift: its yellow light has been stretched to red wavelengths. The light from the nearer, slower-moving galaxies is redshifted less — to the orange region of the spectrum.

2 RECENT PAST
The empty space between the galaxies is expanding, pulling the individual galaxies apart like dots on an inflating balloon. The more expanding space there is between a galaxy and the Milky Way, the faster the galaxy moves away from us.

1 FAR PAST
Waves of light, shown as peaks and troughs, are heading toward the Milky Way (left) from three other galaxies. The light starts out at the wavelength of yellow, but the light we receive is redshifted, as shown by the colors.

As space expands, the galaxies are pulled apart from one another. Note that all the galaxies are moving apart from one another. If you lived on any of these galaxies, you would think you were at the center of the expanding Universe.

HUBBLE'S LAW

Hubble measured the redshift (which gave the speeds) and brightness (which gave the distance) of many galaxies. When he drew up a graph of the redshift against the distance, he found that the galaxies lay on a straight line: the speed at which they were receding was proportional to the distance. This discovery is enshrined as Hubble's Law. The expansion rate, the Hubble Constant, is being measured ever more precisely: it is now thought to be about 12 miles/sec (20 km/sec) for each 1 million light-years.

The amount a galaxy's dark spectral lines shift toward the red wavelengths indicates the speed the galaxy is moving away from us.

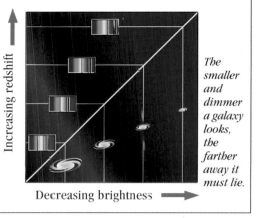

Increasing redshift →

Decreasing brightness ➡

The smaller and dimmer a galaxy looks, the farther away it must lie.

WINDING THE FILM BACKWARD

After Hubble discovered the expansion of space in 1929, astronomers were prompted to "wind the film backward": if the process of expansion is reversed, it leads to the conclusion that the Universe began in an explosion. The rate of expansion, the Hubble Constant, tells you how long ago the explosion occurred. Early estimates of the expansion rate were high, giving an age that was younger than the Earth. Nonetheless during the next 20 years, most astronomers came to believe the Universe began in some kind of Big Bang.

Steady state theory

The idea that the Universe had a definite beginning did not appeal to all astronomers. In 1948, Fred Hoyle, Hermann Bondi, and Tommy Gold came up with the Steady State theory. For them, the Universe had no beginning, and no end. Although expanding, it stayed in perfect balance – like a pool kept full to overflowing by a trickle from a water faucet. The "faucet," in this case, is the continuous creation of matter from energy – at the paltry rate of less than one atom per cubic mile of space per hour.

Most famous of the Steady State trio is the British cosmologist and astrophysicist Fred Hoyle, who first determined how stars make new elements. He also writes science fiction.

Hermann Bondi (1919-)

Fred Hoyle (1915-)

Tommy Gold (1920-)

PAST

According to the Steady State theory, the Universe should remain unchanging over time, even though it is expanding. This is a view of the Universe at one instant of time: it is evenly spread with 18 galaxies.

PRESENT

This is a view of the same part of the Universe. There are 18 galaxies, but they are not all the same ones. The original galaxies have moved apart as the Universe expanded, and newly formed galaxies (coded orange) have appeared in between.

FUTURE

Later still, and the scene remains essentially unchanged. More of the original galaxies (coded white) have been carried out of the frame by expansion. But new galaxies (coded green) have formed to take their place.

WHY THE STEADY STATE WILL NOT WORK

The most controversial aspect of the Steady State theory was its dependence on continuous creation: even though the amounts were tiny, it defied the laws of physics. The theory was dealt a fatal blow in 1965, when the background of cosmic heat radiation was discovered. With its extreme smoothness, it is hard to believe it is anything other than the afterglow of the Big Bang. But even before, there were doubts. The abundance of helium exactly fit Big Bang predictions. And radio astronomers had found that galaxies were more crowded together in the past, meaning that the Universe was not unchanging.

How old is the Universe?

TODAY, THE VAST MAJORITY OF ASTRONOMERS agree on the origin of the Universe: all the evidence points toward a hot Big Bang. The controversy in the 1950s and 1960s about *how* everything began — in a Big Bang or as an unchanging Steady State — has been replaced by one about *when* the Universe started. The answer is now within reach. Despite newspaper headlines claiming that astronomers have discovered stars older than the Universe, several different methods of measuring the date of the Big Bang are coming to a surprisingly close agreement given the difficulty of dating something that happened billions of years ago.

Measuring the age of the Universe

Astronomers can measure the age of the Universe in three ways. The first involves "winding back" the expansion of the Universe to find out when it started expanding. The next method is to check meteorites for radioactive elements that have been produced in stars since the Big Bang and are constantly decaying at a known rate. The third technique involves studying stars in old clusters in the Milky Way, born soon after the Universe itself. None of these methods is absolutely precise, but the overlap in their answers is itself strong evidence that the Universe had a definite starting point. Taking an average of all three puts the age of the Universe at 13 billion years.

GRAVITY APPLIES THE BRAKES

Astronomers cannot age the Universe by simply reversing its current rate of growth unless they are certain that it has always been expanding at the same rate. In fact, gravity must be slowing down the expansion all the time: the mutual pull of all the galaxies on each other, plus the attraction of dark matter, acts as a brake on the expansion. The amount of dark matter suggested by the theory of inflation (see pages 12-13) gives an age one-third less than you find by simply backtracking the current rate at which galaxies are moving apart.

Assume a constant speed for expansion, and the age of the Universe would be 17 billion years.

Allow for gravitational brakes, and the Universe is 11 billion years old.

As we "wind back" the movie toward the Big Bang, the Universe grows steadily denser and hotter.

The far-seeing eye of the Hubble Space Telescope can detect the farthest galaxies in space. Its main task is to measure the age of the Universe.

Although the galaxies move apart from one another, the gravity of a galaxy stops the stars within it from moving apart.

The Universe today consists of a network of superclusters of galaxies, gradually moving apart.

ACCORDING TO THE HUBBLE CONSTANT

For more than 60 years, astronomers have been trying to measure the rate of the expansion of the Universe (the Hubble Constant) — which tells when the Big Bang took place. Early measurements gave an age that was far too low. Now that powerful telescopes can reach many distant galaxies, astronomers are confident that the rate they are measuring is far more accurate. It gives an age of about 11 billion years.

The first estimates of the Hubble Constant were 10 times higher — 120 miles/sec (200 km/sec) every million ly.

The Universe is currently expanding at the rate given by the Hubble Constant — 12 miles/sec (20 km/sec) every million light-years (ly).

Allowing for gravitational braking, the Universe's growth makes it between 8 and 14 billion years old, with an average of 11 billion years.

The age of the Universe estimated by meteorite dating comes out at an average of 15 billion years – with the upper and lower limits at 18 and 12 billion years.

18 by

15 by

Looking at the colors of the stars in old star clusters gives a Universe between 12 and 16 billion years old, the average being 14 billion.

11 by

10 by

9 by

8 by

7 by

A newly born globular cluster is a blazing ball of young, hot blue stars.

6 by

5 by

4 by

3 by

A middle-aged globular cluster contains a mix of stars: young blue stars, middle-aged yellow stars like the Sun, and a few red giants.

2 by

Why the sky is dark at night

Heinrich Olbers (1758-1840) was a German doctor and amateur astronomer who posed the simple, yet devastatingly perceptive question "Why is the sky dark at night?" The answer to Olbers's paradox, as it turns out, had implications for both the geography and history of the Universe.

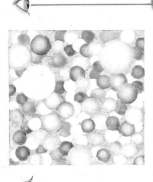

If the Universe did not begin in a Big Bang, and is infinitely old, the sky at night would be ablaze with light. Everywhere you looked, your line of sight would hit a star's surface. In an infinite Universe, there are no dark gaps.

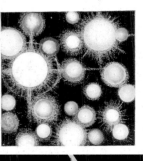

In a Universe that began in a Big Bang, there is a point in the past before which stars did not exist. Your line of sight will eventually reach this black void – which is why the sky between the stars is dark. It is yet more proof that the Universe is not infinitely old.

COLORS OF CLUSTERS PROVIDE CLUES

The Milky Way is surrounded by a "halo" that contains the oldest objects in the Galaxy. Among them are 100 globular clusters, tightly packed balls of up to a million old red stars. But these globular clusters were once young, with hot blue stars. The blue stars have turned to red giants as they have grown older. Astronomers know the rate at which stars age, so the number of red versus blue stars reveals the age of the cluster. The average age is around 14 billion years, with a possible uncertainty of 2 billion years.

Present-day globular clusters contain few blue stars. Nearly all their stars have aged to become red giants.

ELEMENTS DATE EARTHBOUND METEORITES

Meteorites that fall to Earth consist of the ashes of stars that have lived and died since the Universe was born. Some of the different kinds of atoms in a meteorite, such as uranium, are radioactive. They gradually decay into stable elements, such as lead, at a steady rate. By comparing the amount of lead created to the amount of uranium still surviving, astronomers can figure out how long the decay has been going on – in other words, when these elements were originally created in the very first stars.

1 by

The Murchison meteorite fell in Australia in 1969; it contains some atoms almost as old as the Universe.

Today

Each horizontal rung on the grid represents one billion years (1 by) back in time.

More than a million stars throng Omega Centauri, the biggest star cluster in the Milky Way and one of the oldest. The properties of old red stars show that Omega Centauri was born more than 10 billion years ago.

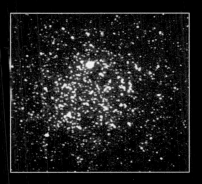

Curved cosmos

WHERE IS THE CENTER OF THE UNIVERSE? And is there an
edge? These two simple questions are among the most
difficult to answer. The Universe may be infinite in size,
going on forever in all directions, and then it has no edge.
In addition, no particular point lies in the "center."
Astronomers call this an open Universe. But in fact space
is not that simple. Gravity can distort the shape of space,
bending it into an unimaginable fourth dimension. It
could even curve right back on itself, as a closed Universe.
Scientists are now trying to measure
the actual shape of the Universe
we live in. It determines how the
Universe continues to expand,
and how it will eventually end.

*The matter that makes up the
huge superclusters and
filaments of galaxies
imposes gentle curves
on the overall
shape of space.*

OUR OBSERVABLE UNIVERSE
Each galaxy is at the center of
its own observable universe,
which is very much smaller
than the whole Universe. This is
the observable Universe around the
Milky Way, stretching 13 billion light-
years out into space — as far as we can see
in the time since the Big Bang took place.

Our Universe: the outside view
This is the ultimate bird's-eye view: how our
Universe may look to a superior being who lives
outside our own space and time. It stretches far
beyond the Universe we can observe from the
Milky Way. This is an open, infinite Universe,
with no center and no edge, but slightly curved
into a fourth dimension. To fit it on the page,
we have had to represent a three-dimensional
Universe in two dimensions.

OBSERVABLE UNIVERSE TWO
A galaxy trillions of light-years away
will also be centered in its own
observable Universe. This, too,
will be 13 billion light-years
in radius, bounded in all
directions by the Big Bang.
But the Milky Way is well
over the horizon, just as
this galaxy is outside
our observable Universe.

ALBERT EINSTEIN ON GRAVITY
In 1915 Albert Einstein (1879-1955) overturned all
previous ideas of space and gravity with the publication
of his general theory of relativity. This says that a massive
body, such as the Earth or a star, bends space near it.
We feel this curvature of space as gravity. The theory
also predicts that there could be a universal
force of repulsion, the "cosmological
constant," operating over millions
of light-years, but there is little
evidence that this force really exists.

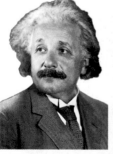

The greatest scientist of
the 20th century, Einstein was
unremarkable at school and
started work as a patents clerk.

*The
curved
grid lines
show the
distortion of
space by matter.*

Empty three-dimensional space can be visualized as a cube.

Put a massive object into space, and the structure becomes distorted.

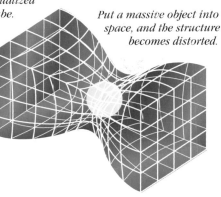

Invisible dark matter – which makes up 90% of the Universe – bends space still more.

Cramming three dimensions into two

Einstein's theory of relativity says that the gravity of an object manifests itself by distorting space. Visualizing space bent by the presence of matter is not easy. The simplest way is to represent three-dimensional space in two dimensions. Imagine empty space as being like a thin rubber sheet on which you place a massive object: it warps the sheet to make a dent, or "gravitational well." The more massive the object, the deeper the well.

If the open Universe theory is correct, the Universe was born infinite in size. However much it expands, the Universe is always infinite in extent.

LOCAL BENDING

This two-dimensional representation shows how space can be bent locally. Here, the Earth distorts space into a well in its vicinity, forcing objects to follow the curved gridlines. We feel the effect as gravity.

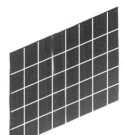

Where gravity bends space, parallel lines can meet and the angles of a triangle need not add up to 180°. The angles in a triangle drawn around the Earth would add up to more than 180° – but only by one part in a billion.

An open, infinitely large Universe could be saddle-shaped. This is called "negative curvature."

A WARPED UNIVERSE

The Earth's gravitational pull corresponds to only a small distortion in space. More massive objects produce much larger distortions. And the combined mass of all the galaxies and dark matter in the Universe can bend the whole of space into a fourth dimension. We cannot comprehend this curvature, but we can illustrate how a 2-D universe could be bent into the third dimension. According to Einstein's general theory of relativity, this bending can result in three possible shapes depending on the amount of matter in the Universe.

If there were more matter, the Universe could be completely flat. It is still infinite.

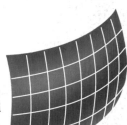

A Universe containing a lot of matter has a "positive curvature." This kind of space could curve back on itself.

The theory of inflation predicts an amount of matter in the Universe that makes it – on the largest scales of all – almost exactly flat.

THE CLOSED UNIVERSE

If there is enough matter in the Universe, space may have enough positive curvature to bend right back on itself. The cosmos we inhabit would then be closed. In this 2-D representation, astronauts exploring a closed Universe would travel right around it without finding an edge. Being unaware of a third dimension, they would be unable to locate a center. For us, living in 3-D space, a closed Universe means curvature into the fourth dimension, with no center in our Universe.

The "expansion of the Universe" means that space itself has been expanding, pulling galaxies apart from one another.

Trillions of years later, the crew aboard a battered rocket awakens to find planet Earth ahead! They have circumnavigated the Universe.

A closed Universe is finite – it does not stretch forever – but it has no edges.

A rocket takes off from present-day Earth in a straight line. The crew, frozen until the rocket reaches an exciting destination, expects to plumb the limits of the cosmos.

Far future

I T MAY APPEAR BOLD, if not downright audacious, to predict the far future of the Universe. Yet this crystal-ball gazing is not as presumptuous as it seems, for the fate of the Universe was sealed at the time of the Big Bang. Once the cosmic clock started ticking, that was that. Crucial parameters that were set during the first few fractions of a second – such as the expansion rate and the amount of dark matter created – determined the Universe's future.

Future of an open Universe

An open Universe will continue to expand and cool forever. It might sound like immortality, but in fact it is a slow, lingering death. Given billions of years, all the stars in all the galaxies will die. Even the supermassive black holes in the centers of the galaxies will not last forever. Ultimately, our frigid dark cosmos will be home to a tiny handful of subatomic particles.

Three fates for the Universe: expansion forever, continuous slowing down, or collapse

Open Universe

Closed Universe

Critical density Universe

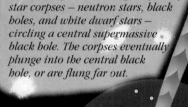

OPEN OR CLOSED FUTURE

The fate of the Universe is inextricably linked to its overall shape (see pages 38-39). If it contains very little matter, the Universe is open: it is infinite in all directions and will expand forever. If there is enough matter to bend space around on itself, the Universe is closed: the Universe will expand but the gravity of the matter will eventually force it to collapse on itself. The theory of inflation predicts a "critical density Universe": one in which there is just enough matter to slow, but not to reverse the inflation.

Today's Milky Way is in its prime. Stars are still being born, and there is plenty of dust and gas around to fuel star birth in the future.

The open Universe after 10 trillion trillion (10^{25}) years: the Milky Way has disintegrated into a graveyard of star corpses – neutron stars, black holes, and white dwarf stars – circling a central supermassive black hole. The corpses eventually plunge into the central black hole, or are flung far out.

It is 1 trillion (10^{12}) years after the Big Bang and the Milky Way has used up all its raw materials. The gas-rich spiral arms have disappeared. Stars are dying; many have already expired.

DEATH OF THE SUN

At 5 billion years of age, our Sun is a middle-aged star. It shines by converting hydrogen to helium in its core – a nuclear reaction that creates energy. But 5 billion years in the future, the Sun will run out of fuel. Its dead core will shrink and heat up, causing its outer layers to billow out and cool. It will swallow up the inner planets Mercury and Venus; and even if it does not swallow the Earth, the heat from its approaching surface will vaporize the oceans and the atmosphere. It will be a certain end for life on Earth.

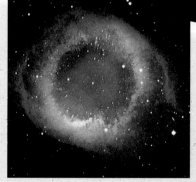

The end: a dying star that has gently puffed off its distended outer layers. The central core will become a white dwarf.

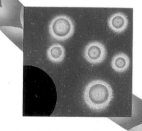

The closed Universe: after 13 trillion years, expansion will stop and be replaced by collapse. Thirteen billion years before the Big Crunch, the Universe is back to its present size. The supermassive black hole in an aging Milky Way is surrounded by dying, old red stars.

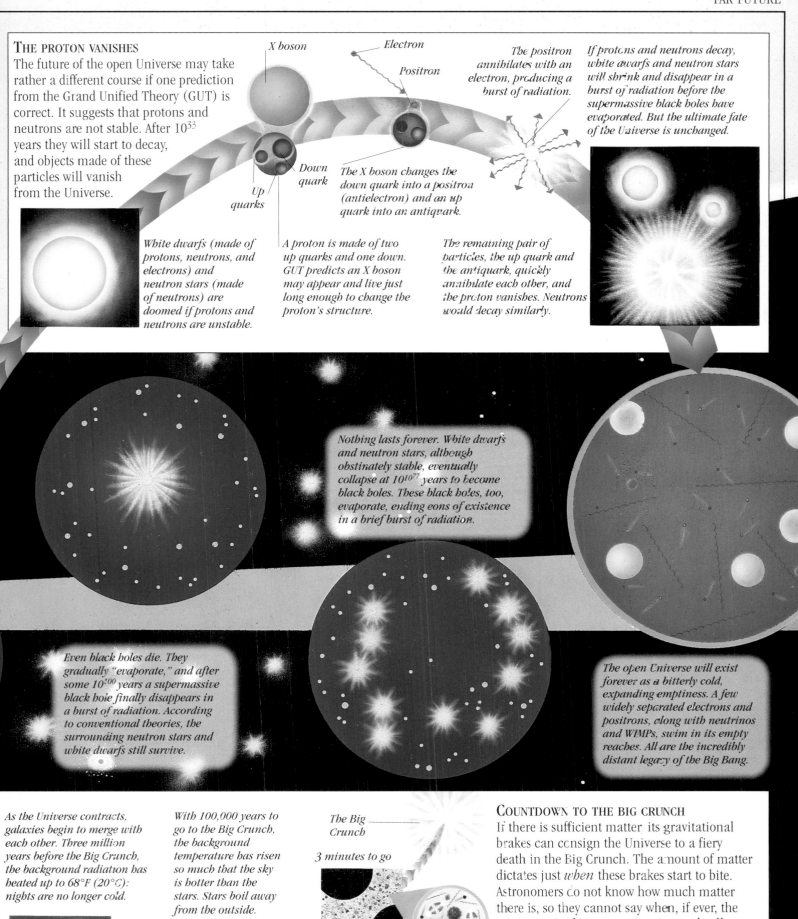

THE PROTON VANISHES

The future of the open Universe may take rather a different course if one prediction from the Grand Unified Theory (GUT) is correct. It suggests that protons and neutrons are not stable. After 10^{33} years they will start to decay, and objects made of these particles will vanish from the Universe.

X boson

Electron

Positron

The positron annihilates with an electron, producing a burst of radiation.

If protons and neutrons decay, white dwarfs and neutron stars will shrink and disappear in a burst of radiation before the supermassive black holes have evaporated. But the ultimate fate of the Universe is unchanged.

Down quark

Up quarks

The X boson changes the down quark into a positron (antielectron) and an up quark into an antiquark.

White dwarfs (made of protons, neutrons, and electrons) and neutron stars (made of neutrons) are doomed if protons and neutrons are unstable.

A proton is made of two up quarks and one down. GUT predicts an X boson may appear and live just long enough to change the proton's structure.

The remaining pair of particles, the up quark and the antiquark, quickly annihilate each other, and the proton vanishes. Neutrons would decay similarly.

Nothing lasts forever. White dwarfs and neutron stars, although obstinately stable, eventually collapse at $10^{10^{77}}$ years to become black holes. These black holes, too, evaporate, ending eons of existence in a brief burst of radiation.

Even black holes die. They gradually "evaporate," and after some 10^{100} years a supermassive black hole finally disappears in a burst of radiation. According to conventional theories, the surrounding neutron stars and white dwarfs still survive.

The open Universe will exist forever as a bitterly cold, expanding emptiness. A few widely separated electrons and positrons, along with neutrinos and WIMPs, swim in its empty reaches. All are the incredibly distant legacy of the Big Bang.

As the Universe contracts, galaxies begin to merge with each other. Three million years before the Big Crunch, the background radiation has heated up to 68°F (20°C): nights are no longer cold.

With 100,000 years to go to the Big Crunch, the background temperature has risen so much that the sky is hotter than the stars. Stars boil away from the outside.

The Big Crunch

3 minutes to go

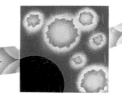

3 million years to go

100,000 years to go

In the last three minutes, supermassive black holes at the centers of galaxies merge.

Radiation breaks up the atomic nuclei: before they turn to particle soup, they are swallowed by black holes.

COUNTDOWN TO THE BIG CRUNCH

If there is sufficient matter its gravitational brakes can consign the Universe to a fiery death in the Big Crunch. The amount of matter dictates just *when* these brakes start to bite. Astronomers do not know how much matter there is, so they cannot say when, if ever, the turning point between expansion and collapse will be reached. But they can calculate what would happen in the countdown to the Big Crunch. It is rather like a reversed Big Bang, but the final instants may differ. While the Big Bang had only mini black holes, the collapsing Universe has supermassive black holes that will survive until the bitter end; the Universe may literally disappear up its own mega black hole.

Other big bangs

W E THINK OF OUR UNIVERSE as being the totality of everything that exists. But if our Universe came into being, why not other universes? If we could step outside our Universe, and dimensions were no problem, we might glimpse a plethora of other universes, populating every dimension. It is a bizarre prediction of modern physics that universes can appear spontaneously, then instantly disappear again. There is nothing to prevent this from happening if the net amount of energy in a universe is zero — a result of the positive energy of all the matter within it being counterbalanced by the negative energy produced by gravity.

Bubbling up from the cosmic foam

If you look at the surface of the ocean from an airplane, it looks smooth. But view it from a rowboat, and the perspective is completely different: there are huge waves, turbulence, and all kinds of violent activity. And it is just the same with space. Seen on the smallest scales of all — less than a trillion-trillionth the size of an atom — it seethes and bubbles like billowing foam. This cosmic foam could be the source of countless baby universes that bubble up from nowhere. Most of them start to expand but never get any farther; well before they reach even the size of a proton, they contract and vanish within a fraction of a second. Each is a tiny closed universe in its own right. But if a universe manages to undergo inflation — like the blue and green universes here — it is set for a long future.

Suddenly, our Universe inflates enormously, propelling itself into a dramatic phase of accelerated growth. After that, its existence is guaranteed.

Our own Universe (colored blue) manages to get farther than its own siblings, and grows steadily.

The multi-dimensional cosmic foam continually bubbles with baby universes. Most expand for a fraction of a second before collapsing and disappearing.

STEPHEN HAWKING'S UNIVERSE

According to the British physicist Stephen Hawking, the Universe originally consisted of four dimensions of space, but no time dimension — and without time, there could be no change. But spontaneously one of the space dimensions turned into time. This gave the Universe the freedom to change and evolve. In this 2-D representation, the Universe starts with three space dimensions. One turns into time and the Universe can start to expand and spring to life.

Now the Universe can change and evolve.

This 2-D universe begins with three dimensions of space and no time dimension. As a result, it is unable to change.

This dimension of space changes into time.

Unchanging universe

When one of the space dimensions turns into time — as a result of fluctuations that take place on the very small scale — the Universe is effectively born, and starts expanding.

Other beginnings

Bubbling from the cosmic foam and Hawking's theory are just two of the ways a universe can be born according to the latest theories of physics and astronomy. Here are two more ideas as to how new universes might be generated.

OSCILLATING UNIVERSE

A universe may emerge from the wreck of a previous universe like a phoenix rising from the ashes. In the "oscillating universe" theory, a closed universe collapses in a Big Crunch. Instead of just disappearing, the matter and energy bounce back as another Big Bang with completely different properties from its predecessor. The cycle may repeat over and over again.

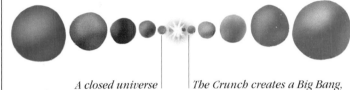

A closed universe collapses, and ends its life in a Big Crunch.

The Crunch creates a Big Bang, and a completely new universe is born on the rebound.

CONSTRUCTIVE SIDE OF BLACK HOLES

Black holes are among the most destructive inhabitants of our Universe: cosmic vortices with such powerful gravity hat nothing can escape their pull. Their gravity deforms space itself, creating gravitational wells into which stars and gas fall – to disappear forever. But black holes may have a constructive side. One theory predicts that the matter disappearing down a black hole may "bud" off the bottom of the well to produce another universe.

Baby universe grows.

Matter sucked into the black hole "buds off."

Gravitational well of a black hole

A baby universe may bud off from a black hole, fueled by the enormous energy generated by the black hole's strong gravity.

INFLATION ESSENTIAL FOR SUCCESS

Most of the universes that bubble out of the cosmic foam are doomed to vanish as quickly as they appeared. Only if they manage to undergo inflation will they survive. The green-colored universe (right) was successful, but it will not necessarily grow to resemble our Universe. With different forces and particles, it may create some very alien objects.

One day, our expanding Universe may collide with another universe like this. No one is sure what the result will be.

WHY THE UNIVERSE IS JUST RIGHT FOR US

Even if other universes exist, ours is special: conditions are just right for us. That is surprising, because the forces of nature are finely balanced: change one slightly, and intelligent life would never have arisen. If gravity were stronger, for instance, stars would burn up too quickly for life to evolve on their planets. According to the "anthropic principle," these forces are chosen at random in each Big Bang. Most universes emerge filled with unstable matter; only in a few are conditions right for life to evolve. The fact that we are here to piece together what happened in the Big Bang, and explore the complexity of the cosmos, may not be coincidence.

Glossary

Definitions of many of the particles and forces found in the early Universe are given on pages 14-15.

ANTIGRAVITY Hypothetical force of repulsion equal and opposite to the force of gravity.

ANTIMATTER Material made of *antiparticles*.

ANTIPARTICLE A particle having exactly the opposite properties to its matter equivalent. A positron, for instance, is identical to an electron but with positive charge.

ATOM The smallest part of an element that can exist. It consists of a nucleus of *protons* and *neutrons* surrounded by a cloud of orbiting electrons.

BACKGROUND RADIATION See *microwave background radiation*.

BIG BANG The violent event that created the Universe, and the whole of space and time. It took place about 13 billion years ago.

BIG CRUNCH Opposite of the *Big Bang*: the ultimate collapse that may take place if the Universe starts to contract.

BLACK HOLE An object with gravity of such strength that nothing, not even light, can escape. Collapsing stars produce some black holes. Others may be supermassive (weighing in at millions of suns) or "mini" (as small as *atoms*).

BLUESHIFT Compression of lines in a *spectrum* toward blue, or shorter, *wavelengths*, caused by a star or galaxy moving closer. It is due to the Doppler effect.

CLOSED UNIVERSE Universe that contains sufficient *matter* to cause it to recollapse.

DARK MATTER Invisible *matter* that reveals itself through its gravitational effects. Although it is believed to make up more than 90% of our Universe, scientists do not yet know what it consists of.

DECAY The process whereby radioactive *element*s and unstable particles change into more stable substances. Also, the manner in which *black*

holes eventually disappear.

ELECTRIC CHARGE A property of *particles* that makes them attract or repel by electrical forces: it can be positive or negative.

ELECTROMAGNETIC RADIATION Radiation made up of electrical and magnetic fields and that moves at the speed of light. It ranges from short wavelength gamma rays to long wavelength radio waves, taking in X-rays, ultraviolet radiation, light, and infrared radiation.

ELEMENT A substance that cannot be broken down into anything simpler by means of chemical reactions.

ENERGY A measure of the capacity to do "work" – more simply, the amount of stored "oomph."

FILAMENT Long string of galaxies enclosing huge *voids* of empty *space*.

FORCE Something that changes the movement or shape of a body.

GAMMA RAYS See *electromagnetic radiation*.

GENERAL RELATIVITY Theory of relativity that describes how *matter* behaves in the presence of strong gravitational fields.

GLOBULAR CLUSTER A dense ball of about a million old red stars. Globular clusters are arranged in a loose framework around galaxies like our own.

GRAND UNIFIED THEORY The theory that seeks to unify the four forces of the Universe – weak, strong, electromagnetic, and gravitational – into one superforce.

HUBBLE CONSTANT Measure of the rate of expansion of the Universe.

INFLATION The sudden, dramatic swelling of the Universe that took place fractions of a second after the *Big Bang*.

INFRARED RADIATION See *electromagnetic radiation*.

LAST SCATTERING SURFACE The surface dividing the young, hot, opaque Universe from the later, cooler, transparent Universe. It

is the origin of the *microwave background radiation*.

LIGHT See *electromagnetic radiation*.

LIGHT-YEAR Distance covered by a ray of *light* traveling at 186,000 miles/sec (300,000 km/sec) in a year. It is about 5.9 trillion miles (9.5 trillion km).

MASS Amount of *matter* making up a body. On Earth, the mass of a body is equal to its weight.

MATTER Anything that has *mass* and occupies space. *Particles* making up matter have exactly the opposite properties to those making up *antimatter*.

MESSENGER PARTICLE Particle that conveys a force. Gravitons, for instance, are thought to transmit the force of gravity.

MICROWAVE BACKGROUND RADIATION The "afterglow" of the *Big Bang* – heat radiation from the *last scattering surface* cooled by the expansion of the Universe.

NUCLEAR FUSION Nuclear reaction in which one kind of *atom* (eg, hydrogen), under extreme heat and pressure, combines to form another (eg, helium). The energy released keeps stars shining.

NEUTRON Neutral *particle*, today found only in the nucleus of an *atom*.

NEUTRON STAR Collapsed star made largely of *neutrons*.

OPEN UNIVERSE Low-density Universe that will continue to expand forever.

PARTICLE A tiny, individual component of *matter*, with a characteristic *mass*, spin, and *electric charge*.

PARTICLE ACCELERATOR Apparatus in which *particles* are accelerated to speeds close to that of light to investigate how *matter* behaves at very high energies – such as happened in the *Big Bang*.

PROTON Positively charged *particle*, now found as the nucleus of hydrogen atoms and part of the nuclei of other *atoms*.

QUASAR Brilliant core of a distant, young, active galaxy, thought to be dominated by a *black hole*.

RADIATION The way in which energy is propagated through the Universe. The most familiar form is *electromagnetic radiation*.

RADIO WAVES See *electromagnetic radiation*.

REDSHIFT Stretching of lines in a *spectrum* toward longer, or red, *wavelengths*, caused by a star or galaxy moving away. Redshifts are used to measure distances to remote galaxies.

SPACE The region between the stars, planets, and galaxies. The shape of space – the way it curves – is determined by the

---

EXTREME NUMBERS

The study of cosmology is the study of extremes. It ranges over wide territory, taking in the limits of size, density, energy, speed, and distance. The numbers it uses reflect this: they are often so mind-bogglingly enormous that it is impossible to appreciate them. In situations like this, it helps to use shorthand. In the case of very large numbers, scientists often refer to a billion (one thousand million) or a trillion (one million million). Really large and small numbers are usually handled by index notation. These are expressed as 10^n, which means "10 to the power n." "n" is the index: the number of times 10 is multiplied by itself. For example:

10^2 is 10 to the power 2, or 10x10, or 100

10^6 is 10 to the power 6, or 10x10x10x10x10x10, or 1,000,000

Sometimes the index is so big that it has to be written in this form itself: $10^{10^{77}}$. Small numbers have negative indices. So 10^{-1} is 1/10 (0.1); 0.01 is 10^{-2} (because it is 1/10x10); a millionth is 10^{-6} – and so on. One special case is 10^0, which is 1.

Index

gravity of objects in it.

SPECTRUM The result of dispersing *electromagnetic radiation* from an object so that its constituent *wavelengths* are spread out. Dark lines, which arise from particular elements present, cross the spectrum at specific *wavelengths*, revealing the composition of an object.

STEADY STATE THEORY Theory, now discredited, that the Universe is unchanging, with no beginning and no end. It is maintained by the continuous creation of minuscule amounts of *matter*.

SUPERCLUSTER A cluster of clusters of galaxies.

SUPERFORCE See *grand unified theory*.

SUPERNOVA Explosion of a massive star at the end of its life.

TIME The interval that elapses between successive events. It is also regarded as the fourth dimension.

ULTRAVIOLET RADIATION See *electromagnetic radiation*.

UNSTABLE The tendency to change from one state into a less energetic one. For instance, radioactive *elements* decay into stable elements; *neutrons* change into more stable *protons*.

VACUUM A space in which there is little or no *matter*.

VIRTUAL PARTICLE *Particle* that comes into existence for a fraction of a second before disappearing again, created by "borrowing" *energy* from the surrounding space.

VOID Huge region of *space* where there are no galaxies.

WAVELENGTHS Distance between wavecrests on any train of *electromagnetic radiation*. Short wavelength radiation (such as X-rays) is more energetic than long wavelength radiation (such as radio waves).

WHITE DWARF Collapsed core of a normal star like the Sun after it has lost its outer layers.

X-RAYS See *electromagnetic radiation*.

A
Age of Universe 36-37
Andromeda Galaxy 16, 31, 33, 34
Annihilation 11, 13, 16-17, 29
Anthropic principle 43
Antigravity 13, 44
Antilepton 15, 16-17
Antimatter 11, 15, 12-17, 28-29, 44
Astronomical unit 32
Atom 12, 13, 20-21, 29, 44
Atomic nucleus 17, 18-19, 20, 19, 44

B
Background radiation 18, 20-21, 28-31, 44
Big Bang, evidence 12, 19, 21, 35, 36
Big Crunch 31, 40-41, 43, 44
Black hole, mini (primordial) 15, 17, 28-30, 41, 44
Black hole, supermassive 24, 30-31, 40-41, 43, 44
Blueshift 34, 44
Bondi, Hermann 35

C
Cepheid variables 33
Closed Universe 38-41, 44
Clusters, galaxies 23, 31, 33
Clusters, stars 33, 36-37
COBE satellite 22, 30
Copernicus, Nicolaus 32
Cosmic Background Explorer 22, 30
Cosmic inflation 12-13, 28, 36, 40, 42, 44
Cosmic string 14-15, 17, 23, 28-29
Cosmological constant 38

D
Dark matter 14, 15, 17, 20, 22, 23, 30-31, 36, 39, 40, 44
Decay 16-17, 41, 44
Density 10, 12, 28-29
Doppler effect 34

E
Earth 25, 26, 40
Einstein, Albert 11, 28, 38-39
Electromagnetic force 13, 14
Electron 11, 15, 17, 18, 19, 20-21, 29, 30, 41
Elements 18-19, 20, 25, 19, 37, 44
Expansion 10-11, 12, 16, 18, 20, 21, 28-31, 34-35, 36-37, 39, 40, 42-43

F
Filament 22-23, 44
Forces 11, 12-13, 14, 44
Fourth dimension 38-39, 42-43

G
Galaxies 16, 22-23, 24-25, 30-31, 32-33, 34-35, 36-37, 38
Gamma ray 17, 20, 44
Gamow, George 18, 25
Gas cloud 19, 22-23
General relativity 38-39, 44
Globular cluster 33, 36-37, 44
Gluon 14-15, 17, 28-29
Gold, Tommy 35
Grand Unified Theory 12, 14, 41, 44
Graviton 14, 28-29
Gravity 11, 12, 13, 14, 22, 24-25, 31, 36, 38-41
Guth, Alan 12, 13

HI
Hawking, Stephen 42
Helium 18-19, 20-21, 22, 23, 25, 29
Higgs boson 15, 28-29
Hoyle, Fred 35
Hubble Constant 35, 36, 44
Hubble, Edwin 34-35
Hubble's Law 35
Hubble Space Telescope 30, 36
Hydrogen 18-19, 21, 22, 23, 28, 30
Inflation 12-13, 28, 36, 40, 42, 44

L
Last scattering surface 20-21, 30, 44
Leavitt, Henrietta 33
Lemaître, Georges 28
Lepton 14-15, 16-17, 28-29
Light 17, 20-21, 29, 44
Light-years 32-33, 44
Lithium 18-19, 29

M
Magnetic monopole 14, 17, 28-29
Matter 11, 12-13, 14, 15-16, 22, 28-29, 39, 40-41, 44
Matter, creation 13, 14-21, 28-29
Matter dominated era 21, 30
Messenger particle 14-15, 16, 28-29, 44
Meteorite 36-37
Microwave background radiation 18, 20-21, 28-31, 44
Milky Way 24-25, 32, 35, 37, 38, 40

N
Nebula 19, 34
Neutrino 15, 17, 19, 20, 22, 23, 29, 31, 41
Neutron 17, 18-19, 25, 29, 30-31, 41, 44
Neutron star 40-41, 44
Nucleosynthesis 19, 25

O
Olbers, Heinrich 37
Omega Centauri 37
Open Universe 38-41, 44
Orion Nebula 19

PQ
Parallax 32
Particle 10-19, 20, 28-29, 40-41, 44
Particle accelerator 10, 16, 28, 29, 44
Penzias Arno 21
Photon 14, 15, 17, 18, 20-21, 28-29
Planets 16, 25, 30, 32, 40
Positron 11, 15, 31, 41
Primordial black hole 15, 17, 28-30, 41, 44
Proton 17, 18-19, 20, 25, 29, 41, 44
Ptolemy 32
Quark 14-15, 16-17, 18, 28-29
Quasar 24, 44

R
Radio galaxy 24
Radiation dominated era 20, 30
Redshift 34-35, 44
Ryle, Martin 24

S
Space 8-9, 10-11, 38, 42, 44
Spectrum 34, 45
Stars 16, 25, 32
Steady state theory 35, 36, 45
Strong force 13, 14
Sun 25, 26, 30, 32, 40
Supercluster 23, 36, 45
Superforce 13, 45

T
Temperature 10, 12, 13, 16, 17, 18, 20, 21, 28-29, 41
Time 8-9, 10-11, 42, 45

UV
Vacuum 11, 12-13, 45
Virtual particle 11, 12-13, 45
Void 22-23, 44

W
W boson 14, 28-29
Weak force 13, 14, 16
White dwarf 30-31, 40-41, 45
Wilson, Robert 21
WIMPs 14, 17, 18, 19, 20, 22, 23, 28-29, 31, 41

XYZ
X boson 15, 16, 28-29, 41
X-rays 20, 45
Z boson 14, 28-29

Acknowledgments

American Institute of Physics/Emilio Segre Visual Archives/Physics Today Collection 18br; /Photo by Dorothy Davis Locanthu 28bl; Ancient Art & Architecture Collection 27cr; Bridgeman Art Library/Bible Society 26cl; /Louvre 26b; Camera Press/John Reader/ILN 24bc; Jodrell Bank, University of Manchester 23 br; Mary Evans Picture Library 27tl; 34cl; /Explorer 34 clb; Massachusetts Institute of Technology/Donna Coveney 12tr; NASA 14cl; Natural History Museum 37bl; Pictor International 14br; Robert Harding Picture Library 27br; Royal Edinburgh Observatory/Anglo Australian Telescope Board/David Malin 40bl; Science Photo Library 16br; 37br; /CERN 29c; /Dr. Ray Clark & Marwyn Goff 22tr; /Dr. Eli Brinks 31br; /Clive Freman, Royal Institution 13cb; /Tony Hallas 13bc; /Harvard College Obervatory 35cr; /Los Alamos National Laboratory 15br; /Cern, P. Loitez 10b; NASA 22bl; /Francoise Sauze 14bc; /Dr. Rudolph Schild 35tr; /Space Telescope Science Institute/NASA 19br; 25tl; 25cl; /Starlight 14c; /Starlight/Roger Ressmeyer 21cr; Werner Forman Archive/Liverpool Museum 27tr.

Every effort has been made to trace the copyright holders and we apologize in advance for any unintentional omissions. We would be pleased to insert the appropriate acknowledgment in any subsequent edition of this publication.

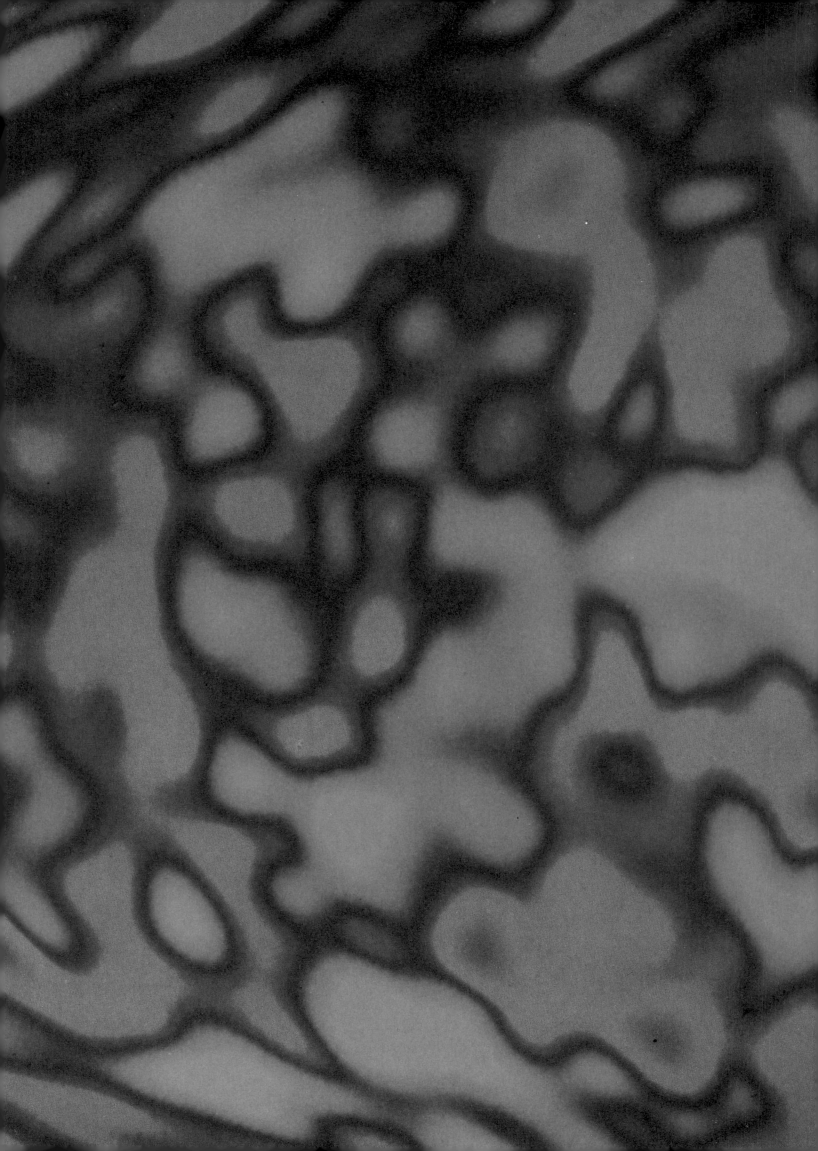